MW01233081

# NO PERMISSION NEEDED

## Unlock Your Leadership Potential and Eliminate Self-Doubt

## Hilda Beaman

**No Permission Needed:**
**Unlock Your Leadership Potential and Eliminate**
**Self-Doubt**
Copyright © 2022

All rights reserved. No part of this book may be reproduced or used in any manner without the prior written permission of the copyright owner, except for the use of brief cited quotations in a book review.

# CONTENTS

# FOREWORD

I wanted to belong.

A casual conversation ensued just beyond my cubicle walls. Accidental eavesdropping revealed the office lunch bunch debating the merits of sandwiches versus salads and who would coordinate the carpool this time. I would be eating at my desk again. It was time to place my order with the local deli. As my fingers reached toward the receiver of my dilapidated desk phone, I realized I was grasping for something else as well. Something that felt just out of reach. Something I had been craving for a while. Something I bet you're hungry for, too.

Success.

For me, success always looked like something external. Something *out there.* Something reserved for other folks. Like the lunch bunch. Maybe it was money, or a job title, or perhaps the "perfect life" (whatever that is—I'm still not sure). But it was always something just shy of my reach. Always something on a timeline … or a deadline … or both.

As the last of the collared shirts heading for lunch disappeared from my view, I made myself a promise. No more lonely lunches. I would somehow work my way into the lunch bunch. Or the "secret success society," as I saw it then.

I became a student of their habits, dedicated to the careful observation of how they—the successful people—dressed, spoke, and interacted. Then I followed their playbook—chapter, line, and verse. I'll never forget how that first lunch bunch sandwich tasted. It tasted like pure victory. Because I finally belonged, right?

Belonged to *what* and to *whom* were the bigger questions. Questions you might have asked yourself at some point. After all, blending in is risky business, often with unintended consequences. Consequences I confronted the hard way after a hiring manager once inquired,

"Tell me about yourself. What value do you bring to this role?"

I froze, unable to answer.

In that moment, I realized that as I strove to dress like everyone else and converse like everyone else, I slowly became indistinguishable from everyone else. Even in my own mind.

The hiring manager's question was a priceless gift. The gift of a powerful discovery I've unwrapped more than once in my career. A gift I want to offer to you if you're willing to accept it.

**Living to your fullest potential is impossible when you're not aware of your value.**

Maybe you've been there, too. Or maybe you're there right now. Maybe you're questioning your value—as well as your values—and feeling uncertain about the answers. What you'll discover in the pages ahead is that you're not alone:

- Many women find it difficult to explain who they are as individuals *and* as leaders.

- Many women are uncomfortable presenting their accomplishments as facts.

- Many women don't know how to explain the values they lead by—their leadership DNA.

- Many women are afraid to walk away from situations that don't align with their values.

I converse with thousands of leaders, executives, and founders globally each year in my role as a tech executive and thought leader. Whether I'm speaking about the future of work or mentoring founders and CEOs, one clear theme emerges. The most valued leaders know who they are and what they value. Without hesitation. And they revisit both definitions on a regular basis.

After publishing two international bestselling books during a global pandemic, I experienced a shift. A shift in what I value. A shift in the value I could offer to others. And a shift in my next aspiration. The quest to articulate that shift led me to Tissa Richards.

Tissa is my valued guide, and I'm grateful she's helped lead me to a powerful truth. The same powerful truth that's the foundation of her success as a tech founder and CEO. A truth she's now extending to you:

**Success begins with your story**

Now Tissa is sharing her blueprint so you can clearly articulate your story, as well as live and lead with it. Its power lies in the fact that it is a story built upon the foundation of *your* values.

I've experienced firsthand Tissa's ability to transform the "raw material" of accomplishments and skills into a compelling value proposition. I've heard the success stories from the leaders she coaches, and I've seen how her immediately actionable tips lead to results. Now it's your turn.

In this book, Tissa will guide you through the same powerful, transformational process I enjoyed, using her F.A.R.E.™ (Fearless – Authentic – Resilient – Effective) framework. You'll learn how to identify, verbalize, and internalize your value proposition. You'll do the same regarding your leadership style and leadership values. And you'll construct a story that represents your differentiated strengths.

The payoff for doing this work is waiting for you on the other side when you actually apply what you've discovered about yourself to your career and life.

You'll become a valued leader as:

- you **fearlessly** advocate for yourself, your team, your value, and your values;
- you **authentically** lead your team to success by being true to your leadership values;
- you handle the challenges of leadership with **resiliency**;
- you deliver consistently and **effectively** on your value proposition.

Thanks to Tissa, I always have an authentic answer to the questions:
Who are you?
Who are you as a leader?
Who are you in your life?

And now you will, too.

Whether you're leading from the backroom or the boardroom, your success starts now. When you turn the page, you will begin to author a new story. *Your story.* The one where you show up in the world as a fearless, authentic, resilient, and effective leader. Enjoy the journey!

KAREN MANGIA, 2022

— Salesforce Executive and Wall Street Journal Bestselling Author of *Success From Anywhere*; *Working From Home: Making the New Normal Work for You*; *Listen UP!: How to Tune in to Customers and Turn Down the Noise*; and *Success With Less: Releasing Obligations and Discovering Joy*

# INTRODUCTION

I magine being publicly fired by a celebrity CEO such as Mark Zuckerberg, Richard Branson, or Larry Ellison. Imagine reliving the humiliation and pain when you're asked about it again and again every time you interview for a job or network with your peers.

Imagine your manager promising you a promotion for nine years and never delivering on that promise, even though you earned it. Imagine being asked by the same manager to mentor other women in the company, helping to prepare them for career progression and promotions of their own.

Imagine being told by management that it's been a tough year, so they'll give you a bonus, but you can't give bonuses to your team members. Imagine having to communicate that news to your team after they've worked overtime to make the company successful despite a faltering economy.

Imagine being fast-tracked to a leadership position and discovering that you can't speak effectively in front of people without hours of preparation or, worse, becoming paralyzed by fear. Imagine having to throw up before meetings—sometimes into a garbage bin (or your purse) if a restroom isn't nearby.

Imagine working for years on the biggest deal in your company's history, earning a bonus that helped you pay down your mortgage when the deal closed, then being told you must pay back the bonus because the customer defaulted on the terms of the contract, and your higher-ups made the strategic decision to refund their money to preserve other elements of the ongoing relationship.

Imagine working hard to secure an amazing executive job, then discovering that your original offer was two and a half times lower than the industry standard for that role. Imagine being too afraid to speak up about the injustice in case the job opportunity disappears.

Imagine winning awards and accolades for doing your job well in a highly respected company yet still feeling unfulfilled at work. Imagine knowing your passions lie elsewhere, but you can't seem to find the courage to make a big change.

Well, people are out there who don't have to imagine these scenarios because they are real, and at least one such scenario has happened to them.

In each case, the women involved didn't know how to handle the situation, and they feared the consequences of speaking up. They worried about their reputations. They felt trapped like flies in the often-sticky web of leadership.

When each woman came to me for help navigating their way out of these dilemmas, I asked them to think about the answers to three building-block questions:

- Who are you?
- Who are you as a leader?
- Who are you in your life?

When each was armed with the answers, they were boldly able to resolve their situations.

The answers to these questions are at the core of nearly everything you need to know to be a fearless, authentic, resilient, and effective leader.

If you are wondering why these people came to me, I will tell you.

I was born with my fist raised into the air, confidently announcing to the world that I was here, ready to roll. *(My mother loves to recount that story.)* Since then, I've announced myself in many other ways and haven't sought permission for anything. *(My mother also loves to confirm this.)*

From the ages of ten to thirteen, I was convinced it was time for Oprah Winfrey to retire from her talk show. I doubted anyone over the age of thirty could keep up with the energy required to host a national television show. I wrote her a series of letters, suggesting I become her replacement. I explained I had the right skills and personality to assume the position. And I very generously offered to make the transition for free. If you're curious, I never heard back from Oprah, and my offer still stands.

That fearless chutzpah endured as I grew up. I became a bold, authentic, and trusted technology founder and CEO. I've established and led multiple companies. Some have been successful, while others have been wildly *un*successful. I wear my signature loud cowboy boots to every single meeting. You could say that I'm an unapologetic extrovert.

I've been in many difficult and uncomfortable situations over the course of my career as a technology executive. I've dealt with unacceptable behavior from stakeholders. I lost millions of dollars when I shut down my last company. I've led teams of people who made great sacrifices to help ensure that my companies are successful. And, I've had to make difficult decisions affecting those teams so that I could stay aligned with my values.

In all these situations, I've learned who I am as a leader and why that matters to me. I've also learned to lead with empathy, curiosity, and transparency. I am not afraid to walk away when things don't feel right or when they aren't aligned with how I lead. Most importantly, I know that few decisions are fatal, either to your career, your confidence, or your future. And as I've learned these lessons, I've become increasingly resilient and effective.

For the first time in many years, I am not running a fast-paced software startup. Instead, I am harnessing my vast experience to run a thriving business that provides keynote speaking, corporate training, and executive coaching. I hold workshops and address global audiences at conferences on the topics you'll learn about in this book. I advise and guide executives and teams from some of the largest companies in the world.

I speak to thousands of women across the nation, across the world, across industries, and across organizations of all sizes. When I keynote at conferences, facilitate corporate workshops, or coach executives, I pose the three key questions mentioned earlier:

- Who are you?
- Who are you as a leader?
- Who are you in your life?

The overwhelming majority of women struggle to answer these questions at first. In many cases, they are taken aback by them. They're so busy being busy—working hard, juggling careers and family life, figuring out what they want from their professions, struggling to put their finger on how to define themselves—they don't have the time, nor do they take the time, to think about these important topics.

Yet, these questions are critically important. The answers reveal fundamental truths about the state of leadership confidence today. As women make huge strides into C-suites and boardrooms, these answers—and what they disclose—have never been more important.

Here's what's behind each question:

**Who are *you*?**
What value do you bring to professional situations? How does this impact you in your career? Why do people come to you, hire you, and work for and with you? What problems do you solve? How do you solve them? Why does that matter? How does this value transform companies and people?

**Who are *you as a leader*?**
How do you activate the value you bring? How do you navigate through the world of leadership to deliver your value in a consistent way? How do you lead other people, and *why* do you lead that way? What values and principles influence how you operate? What are your non-negotiables?

**Who are *you in your life*?**
Are you living your leadership potential and values in all situations? Are you happy, resilient, and fulfilled? Are you confident and fearless without needing anyone's validation or permission? What is your purpose? What legacy will you leave with your leadership?

As you can see, I consciously chose the title of this book, *No Permission Needed,* for a reason. Various dictionaries define *permission* as the act of giving formal consent or authorization for someone to do something, or for something to happen. Permission, no doubt, is an aspect of leadership. But this definition is externally focused. By contrast, this book explores the *internal* side of leadership. It's about **you**. How do **you** want to lead? How do **you** want to live your life?

You don't need permission to be you. You don't need permission to deliver your value. Nor do you need permission to live or lead in a way that is aligned with your values.

**Yet every year, I speak to, coach, and train thousands of women who feel as if**

**they *do* need permission.** They hesitate or hold themselves back from their full potential. They seem to be seeking external authorization—the go-ahead to even answer the questions I ask of them. This constant searching for a nod of approval holds them back from embodying their potential as confident, effective individuals and leaders.

Here are common themes I encounter when I speak to women around the world. Do you see yourself in these women?

- They are afraid of failure.
- They sometimes feel like an impostor.
- They don't know the value they bring to the table.
- They don't know the values that guide them.
- They don't know how to communicate either their value or values to others.
- They don't have the confidence to tell the world who they are.
- They have trouble answering the questions, "Who are you?" "Who are you as a leader?" and "Who are you in your life?"

But what if you could wave a magic wand and change those patterns of behavior? What if you could replace your hesitance with fearlessness, authenticity, resilience, and effectiveness?

Do you really need permission to be you? Permission to lead your own way? Permission to live your life as you see appropriate?

I am here to tell you the answer is a resounding NO.

Permission already exists. It's inside you. You just have to access and activate it.

If you are still wondering why you should give this approach a try, I can imagine the reasons for your reluctance. It's easy for me to suggest that you just access and activate your internal permission. I'm a fearless redhead who hasn't needed permission for anything since birth. I'm not living your life. I don't know your struggles or challenges. But here's what gives me the audacity to lead without asking permission and to suggest that you do as well: I have worked with thousands of women, and in the process, I've developed a clear, straightforward way to unlock your leadership strengths. I've seen that it works, so I wrote this book to share the keys with you too.

This book is about you. Your leadership. Your life.

- On the topic of **you**, we'll uncover the unique value you bring and why it matters. After you've identified and articulated your value, I will insist that you fully embody and internalize it. If you believe it, so will other people.

- On the topic of **your leadership**, we'll explore how you lead and deliver your value. Just as importantly, we'll delve into why you choose to lead that way. Your operating values and principles are a vital part of your leadership DNA. When you know this, you can lead effectively, deliver value, and be consistent and resilient no matter the situation or challenge.

- On the topic of **your life**, we'll set you free, armed with the knowledge about you and your leadership, so you can activate and achieve your maximum leadership potential in all situations, at all times. This is how you live your leadership promise daily. It's how you make hard decisions easily. How you effortlessly become fearless, authentic, resilient, and effective in all that you do.

## HOW EXACTLY WILL WE DO THIS?

The practical, transformational leadership framework I've developed has helped people just like you unlock their potential. I take leadership teams at Fortune 500 companies, hyperscale startups, and cohorts of business owners on this journey every day, and now I am taking you on the journey as well. Through self-reflection and a series of straightforward challenges, we'll surface the answers to the first two questions, "*Who am I?*" and "*Who am I as a leader?*" and we'll apply those answers to a variety of challenging situations to answer the larger question of "*Who am I in my life?*"

This framework is called F.A.R.E.™ Leadership. By now, you may already guess that F.A.R.E.™ stands for: Fearless, Authentic, Resilient, Effective leadership.

Let's break it down.

**Fearlessness** unlocks your authenticity.

**Authenticity** unlocks your resilience.

**Resilience** unlocks your effectiveness.

**Effectiveness** unlocks and activates your optimal leadership potential.

As you embark on your F.A.R.E.™ leadership journey, remember that you are always the one behind the wheel, driving your own success. After reading this book and completing the challenges contained within it, you'll be ready to lead your own way. And you won't need anyone's permission to do it.

The last section of this book includes a series of challenges. Ready to go deeper and want a place to answer the challenges on your own? Follow the link below to access Tissa's signature challenges—questions designed to help you apply the F.A.R.E.™ framework to your own experiences— as an interactive PDF workbook.

www.tissarichards.com/nopermission workbook

# PART ONE

## YOU

# 1

# RECOGNIZE THAT YOU ARE THE KEY

Just as I was beginning to write this book, Margaret, one of my many CEO clients, had a breakthrough. We had been working together to identify her secret sauce —what it was that made her repeatedly successful in so many companies in a variety of industries. We crafted a powerful statement that took her breath away because it resonated so strongly with her. Margaret told me, "It's the most accurate and powerful thing I've ever read about myself, but I can't bring myself to say it out loud."

*What?!*

Margaret apologized and told me that while she knew the description was spot-on, she couldn't possibly speak about herself so boldly and powerfully.

Naturally, I didn't give up. I knew we'd get her there eventually. After all, the most foundational element of this journey is to clearly know—and truly believe in—the value you bring to every situation. If you don't know and acknowledge that value, no one else will. No other individual will do this discovery work for you. You need to step forward as a leader, spend thoughtful time looking deep inside yourself, then find and enact the answers. It's truly transformational work.

Over the next few chapters, we'll follow a simple, three-part framework I developed. I call it the "Three I's":

1. **Identify** the essence of who you are, the value you bring, and why it matters.

2. **Internalize** it so you believe it and eliminate self-doubt.

3. **Inform** your stakeholders so everyone around you knows.

Each "I" is equally important. If you can't answer "Who are you?" a dangerous vacuum forms in your head and heart. I see those vacuums fill up time after time with the dust of fear and self-doubt—dust stirred up by the awful impostor syndrome and the ceaseless habit of second-guessing ourselves. We throw the term impostor syndrome around casually, but it's real, and it impacts leaders in an incredibly tangible way. Look at Margaret. It took us a while to work through the internalization step before she was comfortable informing people of who she is. Now, she confidently owns her value in a public way.

Before we discover 1) who you are, 2) the value you bring, 3) how to internalize that value, and 4) how to confront your case of impostor syndrome head-on, here are a few examples of people who wrestled with these issues and prevailed.

## Brenda's Story

Brenda is a smart, outgoing technology executive who has lived and worked all over the world with her family. She came to me for guidance after a well-known "celebrity" CEO publicly fired her.

In the wake of this firing, she was grappling with the raw emotions of the situation: humiliation, embarrassment, and feelings of failure. These were magnified by the prominent status of the CEO and the high-profile nature of her role.

Adding to this was the practical fallout from the situation. Each time Brenda interviewed for her next position, she was asked to explain what had happened. Recruiters and new prospective employers wanted details. She felt like she was in the movie *Groundhog Day*. She was forced to relive the experience over and over again.

Two consequences plagued Brenda, and she needed help getting past them. The first was the time the interest in her firing took up in interviews. That time should have been spent focusing on what Brenda brought to the roles she was there to talk about. The second was how much space the topic occupied in her head. She was repeatedly reminded of an experience that represented only a tiny fraction of her professional life. As a result, it had become magnified way out of proportion.

We had to get control of the situation by answering the first fundamental question: "Who are you?"

Together, we identified what Brenda brought to the table and the outcomes she had created in her previous roles. We also created a narrative she used to take control of every interview and professional interaction. She opened by saying, *"You're probably curious about what happened with CEO "'X.'" Here's the story in fifteen seconds. Now, let's talk about the value I can bring to this role."* (Or, if she was in a networking situation, *"Now, let's talk about the kind of role I'm looking for."*)

Our strategy worked perfectly. Only a few people wanted to dig further. We role-played how to deflect those questions and return the conversation back to where it belonged: to her value and how it applied to the position in discussion.

Brenda now has a great role at a Fortune 50 company. The experience with her former CEO is rapidly receding in others' minds and is barely visible in the rearview mirror of her own consciousness. The tools we equipped her with—clearly knowing who she is, controlling her narrative, and leading with her value—remain fresh in her mind.

## Eryn's Story

Eryn is a bubbly, outgoing marketing specialist who lives just outside Austin, Texas. When we met, she had recently taken an exit package from a large Fortune 100 technology company. She had worked there in a variety of roles since graduating from college more than twenty years earlier.

After taking the package, Eryn suddenly found herself in a position she hadn't been in for a long time. She had to tell recruiters, her network—even herself—what she was good at and what she was looking for next. She had to answer the question, "Who are you?" and she had to do it quickly.

In a large company, it is common for momentum to drive success. When you effectively initiate or complete projects, you are often automatically rolled into bigger and higher-profile roles. Internal recognition and processes, combined with that momentum, replace the need to articulate *how* you successfully deliver in your roles. You don't need to articulate "Why you" in order to rise rapidly, since your successes frequently speak loudly and sufficiently for themselves. That is, as long as you are not applying for a role outside of the company.

But now that Eryn was seeking a position with a new employer, she and I had to get to work. We took twenty years of her accomplishments and determined what they meant. We set out to answer the questions about who she was now, her value proposition, and the types of roles she should look for. We assessed her skills and accomplishments and asked, "So what?" about each of them. Quickly, a theme emerged. She was trusted by her enormous organization to operationalize global brand and technology initiatives, ensuring they rapidly converted to revenue.

Armed with the *aha!* of her value proposition, Eryn saw her work in a clearer light. She aligned her materials—her resume, LinkedIn profile, and messaging to recruiters —and rapidly found a new role in a completely different industry. Today, Eryn is settled in and thriving.

## Holly's Story

Holly lives in Florida with her husband and daughter, and she volunteers for multiple charities. She was a top performer at a global Fortune 50 technology company when we first started working together.

Despite regularly winning awards and recognition for orchestrating major initiatives at the company, Holly didn't feel fulfilled or happy. She kept imagining starting her own business. But she quickly shut down those thoughts, knowing she had a good job at a great company and a young child to support at home.

Despite her professional successes, Holly found it hard to answer the question, "Who are you?" So I asked her to walk me step by step through the projects and initiatives she led at work. That exercise showed that she is skilled at aligning big teams around audacious ideas and goals to drive revenue. We brainstormed where else she could create an impact with those skills. Holly confessed that her passions lay with women and minority-owned small businesses— businesses with enormous potential; businesses that need a visionary to help make the right strategic plays; businesses that need a success quarterback.

As we'll address in later chapters, it is important to align your core values with your core passions. Once Holly realized she was doing the same thing in her present role as she wanted to do for these small businesses, she knew her dream was achievable. This lightbulb moment helped free her of her fears. During our first coaching session, she said something that struck me: *"I'm more afraid of success than I am of failure."* None of my clients had *ever* said that before. Now that Holly was newly armed with the knowledge of her value *and* her passion, she was ready to abandon that fear. She took the leap, leaving the safety of her longtime job in corporate America— during the pandemic, no less—to launch and run a company called Success Quarterback.

She's been successful since Day One, and she has never looked back.

## WHY DID I TELL YOU THESE STORIES?

Well, Brenda, Eryn, and Holly's journeys all have a fundamental thread in common. Each woman took the time to ask herself, "Who am I?" and identified why it mattered. She formed the answer into a strong message, internalized it, and communicated it to the world.

It was transformative for each of them. It gave Brenda the confidence to control the narrative about her exit from her previous job in her interviews. It gave Eryn clarity about what she had been doing for the past twenty years and why it was valuable. It gave Holly the courage to take the leap from a steady corporate job and kickstart a successful company.

Beginning with the next chapter, we'll engage you in the same process.

# 2

# FRAME YOUR STORY

When I ask leaders to answer the question, "Who are you?" I usually hear a long—very long—description of what they do. And when I say *long*, I'm not kidding. I've clocked these introductions at an average of three and a half minutes and up to seven minutes at times! Many people include a list of accomplishments, job titles, and companies where they've worked. "I'm Sarah. I do this. I previously did that, and I was also at this company, managing this project. I report to that person. I have this skill. Oh, I've also done this and this. Did I forget to mention my role at company XYZ? I'm really hoping to do this, which is why I do this, and I'm really passionate about this other thing too ..."

[YAWN.] If you close your eyes while listening to someone narrate their resume, it's just like being told a bedtime story. It lulls you to sleep. It's not compelling at all. And it certainly doesn't answer the question of "Why you?" Why should *anyone* pay attention?

After asking this question to thousands of leaders across the world, from CxOs of Fortune 500 companies to the founders of hyperscale startups and the owners of small businesses, I'm no longer surprised by their protracted, unfocused elevator pitches. We are all deeply engaged in the day-to-day aspects of doing business. We're operationally focused on what we have to do and how we'll do it. Our responsibilities make it difficult to pivot to more introspective and compelling discussions.

I know you've probably been advised at some point to have an elevator pitch at the ready. But if you've ever heard me speak or attended one of my workshops, you know that elevator pitches make me break out into actual, legitimate hives. (I always carry an EpiPen due to food allergies; I presume it protects me against a random, seven-minute spiel too!) These pitches are so generic, so long, so unfocused, so ... boring.

Even when someone manages to be brief, it's rare when they successfully answer the question, "Why you?"

## Kathleen's Story

When I first met Kathleen, she introduced herself to me as a Chief Customer Officer of a large SaaS (software as a service) company. She had a relatively punchy elevator pitch about how she delighted customers with customer care programs. It was brief but underwhelming because it didn't get to the heart of her work. I kept asking her, "So what?" Why did it matter that her company's customers were delighted? What was her role *in service to?* Were the company's board of directors meeting quarterly in angst about customer delight or the lack thereof? I suggested that the board was more likely focused on the fact that delighted customers tend to buy more product. This results in recurring revenue and higher margins, which, in turn, drives the company's stock price much higher.

Bingo! Suddenly Kathleen isn't just about customer delight. She's about the outcomes driven by *creating* customer delight. Now when Kathleen introduces herself, she focuses on the outcomes she creates and the value she drives. She is a Chief Customer Officer who drives recurring revenue, high margins, and shareholder value for SaaS companies by strategizing and operationalizing customer programs. When she later interviewed for a new role, she spoke confidently about her broader business value and advocated for higher compensation, positioning herself in the context of the company's success as a whole.

Leaders who spearhead "digital transformation" can learn something from Kathleen's example, too. I regularly speak with Chief Technology Officers (CTOs) and Chief Information Officers (CIOs), and almost 100 percent of them rank digital transformation as the highest business value they bring. I ask them to imagine a board meeting. Has any board member ever said, "You know, what we need is some digital transformation around here!" (Hint: The answer is no!) I ask them to think instead about what challenge they are actually solving. Are they assuring a competitive advantage? Faster time to market? The ability to innovate more quickly or securely? When they speak about their value in those terms, others take them far more seriously—and more importantly, they take themselves far more seriously. As a result of speaking confidently about the business value they create, these leaders are now securing public board positions and catapulting themselves into much larger roles.

So, how do you go from an elevator pitch that shoehorns everything you've ever done (but doesn't say anything about the actual value you bring) to a compelling message that clearly tells people why you matter?

Believe it or not, you learned a useful technique for doing that when you were in elementary school. Remember the classic reporter questions: Who, What, Where, When, Why, and How? Those questions teach us that if you want to tell a good story, you have to ask the right questions. When I help people elevate their elevator pitches to a much more engrossing message, I borrow a few of those reporter questions to get right to the point.

When you identify the value you bring, you need to answer:

- *Who* do you help?

- *How* do you help them?
- *So what?*

The most important of these is the last one: So what?

Remember Kathleen, who "delighted" customers? Or the many CIOs and CTOs who led "digital transformations"? Why are they doing that? What is their work in service to? To be memorable and impactful, you need to be able to say *why what you do actually matters*. When you can answer the *so what,* people will understand why you have credibility and value.

You can break each question down in a bit more detail to get to your own *so what*.

*Who* do you help?

- Who are your stakeholders?
- What are they struggling with or trying to accomplish?

*How* do you help them?

- What do you do that solves their problem or challenge?

- What have you done over and over that makes you valuable to the people or organizations you help?

*So what?*

- Why does what you do matter?
- What is the outcome when you deliver your value?
- What problems do you solve?
- What blockers do you remove?
- What growth do you enable?
- How do you drive change or transformation?
- Why do people care about your results? (Which, of course, is another way of asking, "So what?")

If this sounds difficult, or if you think you may not have a value proposition, read this next sentence twice. **You have a value proposition.** If you didn't, you would never have been hired or promoted throughout your career. Look at your resume. If you have any skills or accomplishments listed there, you are ready to surface your value proposition. I also want to assure you that if you've ever had a hard time identifying that value proposition, you are not alone.

When I keynote at conferences or facilitate workshops and I ask audiences the question, *"Can you identify the value you bring?"* more than 70 percent of attendees respond "No." If this surprises you, it shouldn't. This is simply not an idea that most of us intentionally focus on. We get into a rhythm of delivering great results and leading teams. Before long, we are working hard on autopilot. Time flies by. We forget to step back and ask the fundamental question, "Who am I?"

Because there is no time like the present, let's take the time to answer the question now.

TRY IT YOURSELF!

**Challenge 1: Create Your Value Proposition**

# 3

# CONNECT WITH WHO YOU REALLY ARE

One of Marie Kondo's rules is to ask if an item sparks joy when deciding whether to keep or toss it. That's not a bad philosophy to apply to work, either.

Deanna is a General Manager of an apparel consulting company, and she casually mentioned that one of her rules is to only work with clients who spark joy. As I work with business owners, CEOs, and leadership teams—especially in the wake of the pandemic—I increasingly notice that many of them are choosing to align the value they bring to work with their larger passions and values. And they are increasingly open about it.

Remember Holly? She won awards at her Fortune 50 tech company but still didn't feel fulfilled by her work. When she took the time to align herself with her passion, which is to help small, minority-owned businesses thrive, she unleashed her real potential and launched Success Quarterback.

As you identify your value, I encourage you to also think about your values and passions. A Harvard study shows that the average CEO works 62.5 hours a week. More of us are working remotely than ever before. Work and home life are bleeding into each other with no clear boundaries. Doing work you love *and* are good at has never been more important. You bring the most value at this intersection. And you're the most effective F.A.R.E.™ leader when your value and passions authentically converge.

## Vicky's Story

I've known Vicky Bevilacqua-True for many years. She is a retail executive and founding partner of Navigate CPG. She helps business-to-consumer companies (B2C companies) and consumer packaged goods companies (CPG companies) scale rapidly and find distribution channels. She was interested in targeting board director service. As I worked with her to identify her value proposition, we felt as if a key element was missing. That's when the subject of her true passion came up. She is keenly interested in helping sustainable, organic, and socially driven brands. She is also particularly drawn to women-run and minority-owned companies. So, we added that messaging as follows: "I have a passion and particular skill for helping sustainable, organic, and socially driven brands, which are often women- or minority-led, find footing and positioning in the market, stand out from the competition, and reach a wider audience."

Vicky has essentially increased her value to stakeholders by aligning her passion with her value proposition and communicating it clearly. Potential clients now know she can help with sustainability audits and packaging impact as well as connect them with mission-driven or women- and minority-led companies. She is more fulfilled, and her value proposition feels authentic. Vicky is a great example of aligning your value proposition with your passion.

---

With a bit of forethought, everyone can spark more joy in their work.

## Challenge 2: Align Your Passion with Your Value Proposition

# 4

# SPARK A REACTION WITH A SINGLE STATEMENT

What if one introductory comment from you could instantly set off a flurry of positive interest and action from others, even in a crowded room? Well, it can.

## Gabrielle's Story

Gabrielle was invited to participate in an exclusive networking event held with the intention of introducing prospective board directors to private equity firms. As the accomplished CEO of a $2B healthcare system, she worried that having only ninety seconds to introduce herself wouldn't be enough time to get her message across. Instead, I challenged her to trim her introduction to just twenty powerful, memorable seconds. I assured her that after thirty people introduced themselves for ninety seconds each, she would stand out and be remembered as the person who knocked everyone's socks off in a quarter of that time. Gabrielle was skeptical, but she trusted me. Spoiler alert: She rocked her twenty-second intro.

---

You've already learned that long elevator pitches give me hives. But I do highly encourage you to have a short, powerful, punchy, two-to-three-sentence MAXIMUM introduction ready at all times. Why? So you are always in control of how you present yourself to the world. It's essential that you communicate your value to others in an impactful, memorable, and meaningful way.

You might remember learning about catalysts in high school science or chemistry class. Catalysts are materials that speed up chemical reactions. I don't want to cause any explosions in this chapter, but I *do* want to cause reactions. Specifically, I want you to prompt and control specific reactions when you communicate your value to the people who matter.

An elevator pitch doesn't spark the reaction we're looking for here. Remember, the answer to "Who are you?" is also the answer to "Why you?" It uncovers a host of other answers. Why should people trust you, compensate you, respect you, acknowledge you as a leader and an authority or expert, remember you, or make strategic connections for you?

This book is about you, your leadership, and your life. It's about fulfilling each of those without seeking permission. It's about becoming fearless, authentic, resilient, and effective. It takes boldness and confidence to identify and internalize your value to the point where you can distill it into a short and powerful statement and share it with the world. I call this a *catalyst statement*, and it is the next evolution of your value proposition.

A catalyst statement prompts three outcomes:

1. How people understand you

2. How people remember you

3. How people act in response to you

A powerful catalyst statement doesn't just explain what you do; it explains why what you do matters. It impacts how you anchor yourself into someone's memory, how they describe and introduce you to other people in their network, and how you automatically pop into their minds when they hear of a synergistic opportunity. It makes you more resonant and effective.

Here's how I introduce myself: "I'm Tissa Richards. I'm a board member and repeat software founder/CEO who has helped countless women be fearless and authentic leaders. I now also speak globally to organizations to help all leaders develop an unshakable sense of self so they can perform at their peak and lead values-based, high-performing teams."

I *don't* mention that:

- I have raised many millions of dollars.
- I hold over a dozen cybersecurity patents.
- I have won awards from some of the biggest technology companies in the world.
- I have built advisory boards and boards of directors with members from Fortune 100 companies.
- I speak to and coach C-level executives from Fortune 50

companies.

- I have dozens more bona fides that could boost my credibility.

## WHY NOT?

Because people tune out. Our attention spans have never been shorter. The answer to the question, "Who are you?" is the highest-level *so what*. It takes confidence to lead with a concise catalyst statement in answer to that question. If people are interested, they can find out the rest online or by reading your resume. Or they can drill down with you by asking follow-up questions.

It is much more memorable and repeatable to introduce yourself with a concise summary than with a long, generic biography or elevator pitch. Think of taglines for consumer brands. You remember them because they are short, sweet, and consistent.

The audiences for your message have a lot on their minds, and it's not their responsibility to understand your message, whether it's your catalyst statement or your update at the weekly status meeting. It's your job to convey it precisely and ensure they receive and understand what you're saying.

Your job is harder because of a concept called *cognitive load.*

You expect someone to listen and understand you when you communicate with them, but the recipients of your communications have many preoccupations. Their brains are processing a huge volume of information while you are speaking. This includes sensory, visual, written, and tonal information, as well as gestures. Depending on the situation, they may be simultaneously doing other activities while you are speaking. For example, in an interview situation, this may include reading your resume, preparing to ask you the next question, or thinking about their response to you.

Your listeners are busy absorbing, cataloging, answering, responding, or objecting. They are also processing information that has nothing to do with your interaction. They may be hungry, tired, or mentally adding items to their grocery list. We receive eleven million bits of information every second but can only effectively process forty bits of information per second in the executive center of our brains.

This is what I mean by cognitive load. Everyone's brain is busy and overtaxed.

People have limited space to hear, understand, and remember your message. How do you reduce cognitive load? By minimizing the resources it takes to hear, understand, and remember your value. Do that with a simple, memorable value proposition.

As a F.A.R.E.™ leader, be purposeful when it comes to communicating your value and ensuring that it's heard and understood. And, have the confidence to be succinct. We've worked hard together to answer the question, "Who are you?" with a brief and powerful statement. Resist the temptation to add your entire biography and all your accomplishments to it. If you've answered the *so what* in your statement and internalized it, it will be plenty powerful. Trust me.

A catalyst statement also gives you the time to:

- **Listen.** When you are attentive in either a networking, meeting, or interview scenario, you can add value by better understanding the situation and by thinking and responding strategically to what is being said.

- **Ask questions.** You'll understand the priorities of others and what's behind their questions or concerns. In job interviews specifically, you'll understand the leadership culture and how the executive team functions.

- **Connect and be memorable.** In all interactions, you'll have more time to connect on a personal level. Once you make a personal connection, you'll build relationships and become or continue to be memorable.

When you develop a powerful catalyst statement, you will be much more noteworthy. Think of the last time you spoke with someone and they interrupted you to say, "You MUST meet so-and-so!" That so-and-so successfully anchored themselves in the person's mind, and meeting you tripped a cognitive switch that reminded them of another person. That's what an effective catalyst statement does for you. My goal with this book is to create a concise, memorable anchor that will cause that same reaction about *you*.

## Challenge 3: Create Your Catalyst Statement

# 5

# BE YOURSELF TO BELIEVE IN YOURSELF

W e strive so hard to be like others in the work environment, but did you know that being yourself holds a great advantage?

## Xin's Story

Xin had been a technology founder and a CTO before deciding to pursue a CEO role. Her accomplishments were wide and varied. She came to me for assistance in developing a narrative that could help her meet her goal. While we worked on a shared document, I saw an intriguing comment: "I'm not comfortable saying this about myself," she wrote. I looked more closely at the text she highlighted and saw that it was about one of her most remarkable achievements. I decided to be cheeky and write back: "This is a fact about you. What will it take to get you

> comfortable talking about it? Let's work on that instead of taking it out."

It might sound a bit forward, but being able to verbalize this truth is foundational to the second "I" in the Three I's framework—internalization. Margaret, as you may recall from an earlier chapter, couldn't bring herself to say her powerful catalyst statement out loud at first. She was afraid to walk into the world with any swagger, even though everything within her statement was based on facts. The amazing women I work with often look to others for permission to establish their value. They are uncomfortable stating that value as a fact. This is what was happening with Xin.

I can't overemphasize the importance of this chapter. I can certainly explain the importance of your value proposition. I can show you how to create a compelling one, and I can give you tips on how to communicate it. But if you don't believe in and embody your catalyst statement in your day-to-day interactions, it won't come across as authentic and true. You'll struggle to handle challenges. And you likely won't remember the value you bring to the table in difficult situations. Remember: fearlessness, authenticity, resilience, and effectiveness are key characteristics of F.A.R.E.™ leaders.

If you can't identify your value, you can't internalize it. If you can't internalize and embody it, you can't credibly communicate it to your key stakeholders. This includes the people you lead, clients or customers, partners, investors, and anyone you interview with. In short, anyone who needs to understand who you are and take you seriously.

After all, if you don't value yourself, why should anyone else?

Why is it so important to internalize and embody your own catalyst statement? Well, when you believe in it, you control the narrative about it. This leaves other people with no room to substitute their own interpretations.

Internalizing your catalyst statement is foundational to the F.A.R.E.™ framework. When you can do so, you can lead with confidence and deliver on your promised value.

Whenever I tell people this, they inevitably ask: *"How do I internalize and believe my* value proposition and catalyst statement?"

This is an important question, and the answer begins with an important reminder: The value you bring is quantifiable. The *Try It Yourself!* challenges in this book are data-driven. You can back up their conclusions with your accomplishments and skills. You know you have contributed to successes and that you bring a specific value. Remind yourself of that and embrace it. This is a critical part of the F.A.R.E.™ leadership journey.

Another question I am asked almost daily by leaders is *"How do I communicate my value in a confident but not arrogant way?"* My answer is simple and consistent with my previous answers: **"The value you bring to the table is an indisputable fact."** That's not arrogant; it's factual. It's also authentic—and remember that one of the characteristics of F.A.R.E.™ leaders is authenticity. Present your catalyst statement as a fact, both to yourself and to other people.

———————————//———————————

**Danelle Barrett, US Navy Rear Admiral (Retired) and author of Rock**

*the Boat: Embrace Change, Encourage Innovation, and Be a Successful Leader, further elaborates on this point:*

"Arrogance assumes you know everything, you have the answers, and you can do things you can't. Confidence means you recognize your limitations, you recognize that you need other people to fill in those gaps, you're happy to take risks, and you're comfortable failing. Your work speaks for itself. Be an expert on whatever you're an expert on. It will boost people's confidence in you, which will boost your confidence in yourself."

When you embody and catalyze your value:

- You focus on, pursue, and excel at what you are best at.
- You are the most effective at bringing value and success to your stakeholders.
- You are properly compensated for your value.

- You are rapidly promoted and progress throughout your career.
- You develop credibility and purpose.
- You become memorable and prompt actions that further your goals.

If you can't identify your value, the headspace where that knowledge should reside will be empty. That empty space leaves room for self-doubt. Self-doubt makes it harder to handle the inevitable challenges of leadership. This is why knowing your value is so critical to developing the resilience of a F.A.R.E.™ leader.

In contrast, when you identify your value proposition and catalyst statement, you replace self-doubt with confidence. This unlocks many benefits:

- You are comfortable dealing with challenging situations.
- You are comfortable stepping up to bigger roles and responsibilities.
- You are comfortable saying yes—and saying no—to a variety of situations.
- You have the skills and characteristics of a F.A.R.E.™ leader.

Internalizing your value is critical, especially in situations that shake your leadership confidence. I'm about to tell you a story that I don't share often. But sharing it illustrates how authentic value propositions and catalyst statements contribute to F.A.R.E.™ leadership.

I founded a startup company several years ago. It was an exciting venture at first. It grew rapidly and it was clear we were on the fast track to success. But ultimately, the executive team and board had to make the difficult decision to shut the company down. The decision was based on fiduciary obligations as well as our commitment to remain aligned with our leadership values. The shutdown cost my earliest investors and me many millions of dollars. The circumstances were contentious and challenging. Emotions were raw. I, and many other people, had put many years and a lot of blood, sweat, and tears into the company.

The situation drained me. For a while, I could not imagine how I would bring value to another company or CEO role. My sense of self was shaken. I had trouble answering the question "Who are you?" The value proposition I had previously internalized was challenged. I realized it was too narrowly connected to my role as a startup founder and CEO, so I reworked my value proposition into a broader one.

During the wind-down, situations arose that tested who I was as a leader. In time, I was able to look back and see that despite those challenges, my leadership did indeed withstand the test. I had remained authentic to my values and advocated for them—and for my team—throughout the whole arduous process.

I internalized my more accurate value proposition and gave myself time to re-energize. I no longer felt frustrated that my company was coming to an end. Instead, I navigated the entire situation with greater grace, strength, and resilience. It was transformational. It didn't take long for my F.A.R.E.™ leadership to come roaring back.

This is a big part of why I'm writing this book. It's also why I encourage you to revisit the answer to "Who am I?" regularly. The answer evolves as you do. If it's off-kilter, or you haven't internalized it, your F.A.R.E.™ leadership will suffer.

Here is another example that proves this point.

## Beth's Story

Beth is a soft-spoken financial industry executive with three children. She's an avid golfer, hiker, and outdoorswoman.

She recently retired and has been interviewing for corporate board roles. We worked together to articulate her catalyst statement and materials, then we role-played to prepare her for her interviews. One afternoon, Beth asked if we could fit in a last-minute session to ready her for an interview with a public company board in need of an audit committee member.

The existing board members were fairly well-known CEOs and COOs of public companies. Beth had been familiarizing herself with their backgrounds in advance of the interview and suddenly felt out of her league. I asked her to tell me in more detail what she was feeling.

*"They've all done a lot more than I have. Their companies are bigger. They are household names. I'm not sure what I can bring that they can't."*

Beth and I started unpacking that concern. I asked her to print out her catalyst statement and put it in front of her. The company needed a board member with her specific skill set. None of those CEOs or COOs could deliver that. She brought a different perspective. Her accomplishments and experiences were no less than theirs. Maybe the transactions she had been involved with had fewer zeros before the decimal point. Maybe she hadn't been quoted in the *Financial Times* quite as often as they had. But she brought value that they didn't and *couldn't* bring, no matter who they were.

I asked her specific questions about the company. What were they looking to do? What were their challenges? Could she help them? Had she done similar work before? Could she join that audit committee and make a difference? The answer was yes.

The only thing that was getting in Beth's way was *Beth*. She had let a vacuum develop, through which self-doubt now flowed. She allowed her perception of these accomplished board members to cast a shadow on her own sense of value. When we sat down and reviewed what she brought to the table, that vacuum started to disappear.

I suggested she leave that printout taped to her screen the next day during the interview.

It would keep a seal on that vacuum of self-doubt. I encouraged her to remind herself that she brings an entirely different answer to the question, "Who are you?" than every other board member. Lastly, I told her that it was not a competition. It was only going to be her on the playing field.

The interview went well, and Beth was offered the board director role. And now, she's in line for the committee chair position.

More importantly, she keeps her catalyst statement printed out to remind herself that no situation needs to be intimidating because she brings her unique value to every table where she has earned her seat.

## TRY IT YOURSELF!

### Challenge 4: Internalize Your Value

# 6

# TELL OTHERS WHO YOU ARE

You've done the hard work of answering the all-important question "Who are you?" by identifying and internalizing your value. You've created a clear and pithy catalyst statement. Now it's time to do what Beth and others I've counseled have done effectively: actually communicate it so everyone knows who you are and what you bring to the table.

Leadership is a series of situations where establishing your credibility is critical. This includes job interviews, presentations, negotiations, performance reviews, and hiring your team.

Without having a compelling catalyst statement in any of these situations, you'll spend too much time educating stakeholders about your credibility. You'll have to keep convincing them of *what* your value is, *how* you deliver it, and why it matters to them (the *so what* in the statement). You won't have time to fulfill more important leadership responsibilities if you must repeatedly go over the same groundwork.

This is why you need to control the narrative about communicating your value.

As I mentioned before, so many women I work with say some version of the following: *"It feels arrogant to state my value so explicitly. Can't my accomplishments speak for themselves? Can't I just let people figure out my value by themselves?"*

Finding a balance between perceptions of confidence and arrogance is crucial in these situations. When it comes to your catalyst statement, you must be in the driver's seat, controlling where the narrative about you is going. You will recall that Brenda effectively controlled the narrative about her much-publicized exit from her last role, and it made all the difference in her job interviews. Remember, your value is an indisputable fact, and there's nothing arrogant about that.

You must be crystal clear about the value you bring to the table. When you leave it to other people to draw their own conclusions about you, all sorts of things can happen. They can draw imprecise conclusions. They may pigeonhole or typecast you, propelling you toward a role you don't enjoy or that you aren't passionate about.

You must also remember that the world and your experiences are fluid, and for this reason, it is important to revisit your narrative and revise it as circumstances demand. Here is a testament from Shar Kassam, Chief Operating Officer of Nasdaq Asset Owner Solutions, about her experience in keeping her value proposition current with the ways she was meeting an ever-changing marketplace.

> "I've always been told I'm an amazing strategist and connector, and I internalized that as my value proposition. It's valuable in the investment industry, where I have great results to show for it, like managing a $30B portfolio as the Deputy CIO of a state retirement system. But it hadn't been resonating with me as my most relevant value proposition. After I left my last role, did some consulting work, and worked with Tissa on the F.A.R.E.™ leadership framework, I realized that my value proposition was shifting.

"I solve problems by connecting the right people at the right time with the right resources and thinking about their problems in a non-traditional way. And the problems I solve are evolving. I'm helping to solve relevant issues in the investment industry, including those surrounding the environment, social, and corporate governance (ESG), sustainable investing, and diversity in the boardroom. These are emerging areas, and they need leaders, definitions, big wins, and solid successes.

"I've been very successful in adjacent areas for decades. People trust me, and they continue to do so as I communicate this newer and emerging value proposition."

Shar's experience should remind you of the importance of revisiting your value proposition and catalyst statements often so you can maintain control of your narrative in a fast-changing environment and highlight your ability to keep pace with—and even anticipate—such important developments.

Not being in control of your narrative can impact you in all kinds of high-stakes situations. Your professional life is full of such situations: interviewing for leadership roles, negotiating for your compensation package, and advocating for your team. In these high-stakes situations, knowing your current value—and making sure that everyone present knows your value—is critical.

Claire Wasserman, the founder of Ladies Get Paid and author of a book by the same name, explains the importance of this in concrete terms:

> "I empower women around the globe to advocate for compensation. A lot of factors go into doing this successfully. You have to be comfortable talking about compensation. You have to know the market and know your numbers. You have to articulate and communicate how you bring value and the precise way that value should be reflected in your compensation. If you can't identify and talk about your value, no one else will quantify and compensate you for it."

This is why it's vital that you learn how to communicate your value effectively, confidently, and consistently.

If relating your value to a fair dollar amount is uncomfortable for you, know, once again, that you are not alone and you can overcome this discomfort, as happened in the following example.

## Susan's Story

Susan lives on the West Coast with her three sons and her husband. She hikes, cooks, and does volunteer work. She's soft-spoken and extremely empathetic and focused. Susan and I recently worked together as she interviewed, negotiated, and then onboarded into a CxO role with a fast-growing technology company.

It was an exciting process. Susan aced her interviews. She conveyed her value, leadership style, and leadership values, and closely assessed the culture of the company and the leadership styles of the company's C-suite executives.

When it came to negotiations, Susan's instinct was to do what many women do: negotiate against herself. The company offered her "X," and she was willing to accept that initial offer. Why? Susan reminded me that she was a first-time CxO, and the company had never had anyone in that role (it was previously filled by a VP). She felt the offer was what she deserved. She also feared losing the entire job opportunity if she countered the offer.

My response was to ask whether the company's expectations of Susan would be significantly lower because she was a first-time CxO or because there had never been someone in the role. After we both laughed, we agreed that the answer was a resounding "no."

We also knew the market standard for the role. When it comes to negotiations, I always engage with an HR expert who has access to databases showing industry norms based on role, sector, company size, and revenue. It gives us a great baseline. The initial offer was clearly well below what it should have been.

I reminded Susan that the company made an offer to her because they recognized her value. They decided to place their trust in her to help take the company to the next level. And the industry comparisons showed the compensation should be far above what they offered.

We negotiated her total comp package to **two and a half times** above the initial offer. We did our homework. And Susan knew, internalized, and confidently communicated her value.

She's settled in and enjoying her new role.

---

As I said, Susan isn't alone in her willingness to negotiate against herself. I regularly encounter practitioners who are clearly undercharging or who are too quick to offer a discount. I've openly pointed out that their rates seem too low or that I'm not comfortable underpaying. Helping someone else advocate for their value is sponsorship in action, and I encourage you to do it whenever you see an opportunity to do so.

Be consistent when you communicate your value proposition and catalyst statement. Practice helps. Do it regularly. When you look for a new role, be explicit by stating it on your resume and in your interviews. Also, communicate your value when you are hiring your team. Ask prospective hires about theirs. Use LinkedIn, your blog or personal website, and other aspects of your digital footprint to amplify your message. Get used to doing so. Be comfortable communicating your value so the people around you can also identify it.

As you get accustomed to stating your value as a fact, it gets easier. Present it in the context of the F.A.R.E.™ leadership framework: delivering your value makes you the most effective leader possible. You deliver your value when you consistently and comfortably communicate what that value is.

TRY IT YOURSELF!

**Challenge 5: Communicate Your Value**

# PART TWO

# YOUR
# LEADERSHIP

# 7

# TAKE A LEADERSHIP STANCE

In the last section, we focused on you—who you are, what your value is, what interests and passions you have, and how to communicate all of that succinctly yet powerfully to stakeholders. In this section, we focus on you as a leader. We explore how you activate the value you bring, how you lead, why you choose to lead the way you do, and how those choices impact your resilience and effectiveness as a leader.

Leading others is a big responsibility. The tone you set and the actions you take cascade throughout your team and your organization. You need to guide your team consistently, authentically, and in alignment with your values. When you choose a role, you need to ensure that the culture of the company and leadership team is also aligned. This way, you can fulfill the promise of your value proposition.

This alignment manifests in who you hire, the culture you create for your team, the behaviors you expect and condone from all your stakeholders, how you structure and run meetings, the ways you communicate, and how you handle conflict or challenging situations. In the upcoming sections, we'll examine these areas in more detail. You'll understand why it's important to identify, internalize, and communicate your leadership style and your leadership values.

I want to emphasize that who you are as a leader has real implications for you. The choices you make and the principles you choose to lead by impact your effectiveness, your happiness, and ultimately, your resilience. You will see this in the following example.

## Leah's Story

Leah is a calm, capable technology strategist who has led some of the biggest consumer brands in the world through complex technology transformations. She has several grown children and travels globally with her husband—partly for work and partly for the love of travel.

We recently worked together to find a CxO role that aligned with her value proposition and her passions. Leah wanted to work with a company that needed her large-scale vision, global experience, leadership style, and focus on culture and people.

We narrowed the field to two positions. Leah made it to the final round for both. The next step required on-site interviews and a meeting with the board and executive team. The interview for one of the roles was particularly interesting. It involved a day-long set of challenges, role-playing, and presentations. It was enjoyable and stimulating. We touched base throughout the morning, and it seemed to be going well.

Around midday, I received a text from Leah. It contained a photo of a sad-looking sandwich, a juice box, and a banana that should have been eaten about four days ago. I replied with a series of question marks. The agenda indicated there would be a group lunch where Leah would have an opportunity to meet with the executive team in a more relaxed setting. Instead, they had suddenly changed plans and sent her to the lobby with a boxed lunch. There was no social interaction. No group lunch. No explanation.

Leah was bewildered. The night before, she was surprised when no one had met her at the airport. There had been no dinner or drinks with anyone from the board or executive team, either. She managed to brush it off, but now lunch had been changed to a solitary sandwich and sad banana in the lobby, and she was left wondering if this decision held some kind of message.

Leah called me on her way to the airport after finishing the afternoon interviews and activities. We decided to proactively withdraw her candidacy for the role. Culture and leadership style are extremely important to her. She would be working closely with the rest of the executive team and the board, and their conduct surrounding the interviews baffled her. It didn't feel collegial or collaborative. It's not how Leah would ever treat a candidate—for *any* role.

As much as Leah loved the technology challenges the role had presented, she was decisive. This was not the right place for her. She accepted the other role she had been interviewing for and never looked back.

What Leah and I both knew—and what you now know—is that when you lead your team in a way that makes everyone feel happy and valued, you'll do more than deliver on your value proposition. Companies that win "best places to work" awards—companies with positive cultures— outperform the overall S&P 500 by 115 percent. There are real benefits to identifying and delivering an effective leadership style.

The most logical question to ask at this point is "Who are you as a leader?" In the next chapter, we'll explore the answer in two parts, asking more specifically:

- How do you lead?
- Why do you lead that way?

Your responses will help you make hard decisions, stay calm and effective in challenging situations, and be a highly effective F.A.R.E.™ leader. Let's dive in!

# 8

# DISCOVER MORE ABOUT YOUR LEADERSHIP STYLE

I know your interest in leadership is keen because you're reading this book and have already completed some of the challenges. This is also how I know that you've likely read at least one of the many books in the marketplace that help you define your leadership style, or you have taken a leadership style "test" with your organization. Because so many great books and programs can help you define your leadership style, we will not be exploring that same territory in this book.

For F.A.R.E.™ leadership, it's not important what your leadership style is called or whether it fits into a category with a recognizable name. It's more important that you can articulate and communicate your personal leadership style. That way, your stakeholders know how you lead and what it means for them.

I want you to be able to describe your leadership style to yourself and to other people in words that feel authentic to you. To do that, ask yourself the following reflective questions:

- Do I prefer a collaborative or a hierarchical style?
- Do I lead by consensus or consent? (There are nuanced differences to these!)
- Am I conflict-avoidant?
- Am I comfortable delegating?
- Am I a perfectionist?
- Do I connect with people using empathy?
- Do I believe that emotion belongs in the workplace?
- Am I comfortable being vulnerable with the people who work for me or with my stakeholders?
- When I think about situations that make me uncomfortable—or, conversely, situations in which I excel

—what is it about those scenarios that make me feel that way?

The most important question to answer in this section is this: *How do I lead?*

Here are stories from F.A.R.E.™ leaders explaining their leadership styles and what those styles look like in practice.

———————//———————

"My leadership style is inspirational and caring. I believe in people, and I identify with their value systems. This manifests in caring not only for people's basic needs but also for their aspirations. I dig deep to understand what makes my teams feel valued and validated, and I also try to understand what currency they receive that value and validation in. I can then craft my communication, compensation, and incentive plans around what makes that individual feel valued."
— *Katina Kenyon, Chief Executive Officer, Tree3*

"My approach to leadership is rooted in my belief that my team does not work 'for' me, they work 'with' me. When I was growing up, my dad ran a successful company, and he instilled this leadership philosophy in me. No matter how well I lead or how well I pay my team, everyone works for their own reasons. They have individual hopes and dreams and intentions for their futures.

"This early lesson from my dad formed the way I lead. To the degree each team member is comfortable, I like to understand them personally. I try to understand what motivates them and what makes them tick. This is especially important in the high-pressure world of audit and assurance services, as we sometimes work extremely long hours. We might work through the night or over holidays and weekends for clients. My team is not doing that "for" me. They are doing it for their own goals, and I am there to inspire them and encourage them.

"Knowing what drives my team is also how I can advocate for them as individuals. For many years, I was the talent partner for our audit practice. That role covers everything from recruiting and hiring, talent development and coaching, diversity and inclusion, performance reviews and compensation, to promotion and launching careers outside the firm. During an economic downturn, we had to make some difficult decisions about who to retain and who we should part ways with. A senior partner happened to be in town on a day we discussed each of our hundred-plus team members in detail to make those hard decisions. He pulled me aside later and remarked that it was impressive and unusual that I knew so much about each of them as people. I knew each of their personal goals, individual potential, and life circumstances. That really helped us make hard decisions with more humanity. That is how I lead, and I cannot imagine leading any other way."

*— Emily Rollins, Board Member and Audit Committee Chair, Dolby Laboratories Inc. (NYSE: DLB); Board Member and Audit Committee Chair, Xometry Inc. (NASDAQ: XMTR); Board Director and Audit Committee Member, Science 37 Holdings Inc. (NASDAQ: SNCE) and Dwolla; Former Board Member, McAfee (NASDAQ: MCFE); Retired Audit and Assurance Partner, Deloitte*

———————— // ————————

"I lead by aligning teams around the same goals. Where I've seen leaders fail is where their interests may not be aligned with the people they are trying to lead. This is especially the case where leadership encourages people to think of the size of the pie as a zero-sum game, which encourages individuals to act in their own self-interest, without regard for the greater good. The greatest leaders are the ones who understand how to expand the size of the pie by helping people achieve success, solve problems creatively, and

maximize their value. That grows the size of the whole pie. That's how I lead and what I have tried to do with my teams."
— *Head of Investor Relations*

———————— // ————————

"I lead with empathy and empowerment. As I was working my way up the ladder of leadership, that's the style of leadership I really valued. When I had leaders who empowered me, I felt safe. I felt like my contributions were valued and I had the most impact in those environments. I want to give that back to my team because I see the most results when I lead this way. This leadership style manifests in several ways. One of those is in how I empower people to make decisions. It doesn't work well if I make decisions for my team. Instead, whoever has the most information about something is the one who makes an informed decision. When people are empowered to make those decisions, they tend to

have an amazing relationship with the outcome: they are accountable and committed to the results and own them. It's very effective."
— *Chetna Mahajan, Chief Information Officer, ZoomInfo*

———— // ————

"My leadership style is based on courage and compassion. Courage is an important leadership characteristic for many reasons. Many of my roles have been high-risk functions, and I believe courage helps you make the best decisions in many of those situations. It doesn't take much courage to choose the easiest answer instead of the best answer. Instead, making tough decisions, being effective during distress, hiring someone unexpected or taking risks for my team comes from a place of courage. And compassion is critical in handling the human element of leadership. Compassion goes a long way when dealing with complex issues, repairing misunderstandings, negotiating, and all the interactions we

have on a daily basis. I believe compassion underpins the collaborative and inclusive way I lead."
— *Melissa Waller, President, AIF Global Institute at Alternate Investments Forum*

———————//———————

Do you see yourself in any of these leaders? Do any of these styles resonate with you? Do they remind you of managers you've enjoyed working with? This section is about how you lead, and there are as many leadership styles as there are leaders. There's no "right" or "wrong" way to lead—there's just *your* way.

TRY IT YOURSELF!

Challenge 6: Identify Your Leadership Style
Challenge 7: Commit to Your Leadership Style

# 9

# EVOLVE YOUR LEADERSHIP AS YOU GROW

When I ask women, "Who are you as a leader?" some answer that their leadership has evolved. I'm always curious to find out how, why, when, and what spurred that evolution.

Just like your value proposition will evolve as you mature throughout your career, your leadership style will also evolve. As I coach leaders and take them through the F.A.R.E.™ leadership challenges, an interesting trend emerges. They realize they lead differently now than they did early in their careers. For some, it's a big change. For others, it is an intentional shift to adapt to the needs of their teams.

I share the following stories with you so you know it's natural and healthy to grow as a leader. If I ask you one, three, or five years from now, "Who are you as a leader?" your answer might be different each time. And that's a good thing!

———*//*———

"For a long time, I believed that failure was not an option. I shared that belief with my team and can remember pepping them up on all-hands calls and before big deadlines by reminding them that "Failure is not an option, so let's get this right!" I look back now and can't believe I said that.

"As a leader today, I believe that failure is the only path to success. I've developed a growth mindset: the more I fail, the closer I get to success. So, if I'm not failing, I'm not trying hard enough. I've also come to realize that failure and success are not opposites. I coach my team to fail early and fail often. I care about their attitudes toward learning and how they approach their paths to success.

"There are a few reasons for this significant shift in my leadership style. Moving from primarily waterfall to agile software methodologies helped me realize that my work as an IT leader is as much about mindset as it is about execution. I've also matured and learned a lot. I've had kids and have watched them learn to walk, fall down, pick themselves up, and fall down again. Before I knew it, they were running. My leadership growth is a combination of maturity, exposure, experience, and learning that I'm much more effective now because I don't fear failure."

— *Chetna Mahajan, Chief Information Officer, ZoomInfo*

———— // ————

"I've intentionally adapted my leadership style based on feedback from my team and a lot of business and communications coaching. We have a lot of process-oriented data gatherers at my company. They need all the available information to understand how I've reached decisions and to support those decisions. In contrast, I'm results-oriented, and I like to move fast. I had to consciously train myself to think about things from my team's perspective. They feel more comfortable when I communicate with intention and walk them through my process.

"I saw a big difference when I shifted to this leadership style. Now, as a company, we codify and write down more things. We explain and document decision-making processes and the decisions themselves. This ensures everyone is clear and aligned on what we're doing, and why.

"I see this as being an adaptive leader. It's adapting to lead my team most effectively. I communicated my style to them, asked them to communicate their working style to me, and we "flexed" into each other's styles to find the optimal one that allows us to excel as a company."

— *Melynda Caudle, CEO, Cooper Consulting*

———————— // ————————

"My leadership style has changed as I've grown and learned. Early in my career, I adopted the style of my previous leaders. I began to realize that I didn't like their style. It was too authoritative and hierarchical. I've adapted and matured my style to more closely fit with the way I like to work. I have always been a results-driven leader. I wasn't overly focused on everyone buying in to the results, as long as we got there. Now, I understand the value of collaboration and buy-in as a leader, as well as being dynamic in leadership style based on the people and the situation to maximize impact on the team."

*— Shar Kassam, Board Director, Audit Committee Chair, Nom/Gov Committee Member, Adit EdTech (NYSE: ADEX.U); Board Member, Foundation Credit Opportunities Hedge Fund; COO, NASDAQ Asset Owners Group*

---//---

As you learn and mature as a leader, you'll adapt in ways that enable you to lead in the most effective manner. This is a critical

F.A.R.E.™ leadership characteristic. But one area will likely remain consistent: your values. The leaders I interviewed for this book agree that their maturing leadership styles remain authentic to their core leadership values.

> "I am a believer in situational leadership, where effective leaders adjust to the individual needs of the people they manage. But your leadership values don't change. They are the principles of your leadership, and they are very constant."
> *— Melissa Waller, President, AIF Global Institute at Alternate Investments Forum*

———— // ————

Take the time to occasionally revisit and redo the leadership style challenges in this book. Notice any changes. This exercise can serve as a checkpoint for your leadership style. When you know your most effective style, you can communicate it to your stakeholders. That's how you create consistent expectations, build productive teams, and select the best places to work. This enables you to lead with authenticity and deliver effectively on your value proposition as a F.A.R.E.™ leader.

# 10

# FIVE REASONS TO COMMUNICATE YOUR LEADERSHIP STYLE TO OTHERS

M any of you may be wondering, *Why should I intentionally identify and communicate my leadership style to others?* Perhaps it's the same tug of war between arrogance and confidence we discussed earlier that has you questioning this advice. Maybe you're concerned people will see it as self-aggrandizing. But there is a good reason for communicating your leadership style: you maximize your effectiveness as a F.A.R.E.™ leader when you do.

Here are five more specific reasons, all of which prove you have the interest of your key stakeholders in mind.

## 1. You Align Leadership and Culture

Communicating your leadership style helps you assess the culture of a company and leadership team. You'll select the best environment to showcase and deliver your value.

> "I always ask my managerial candidates about their leadership style, and I ask them to give me specific examples to show me how that leadership style plays out. I want to get a good feel for how they operate and whether they'd be a good cultural fit for both the executive team and the organization. This is important for the candidate's success and the success of the organization. Depending on the examples they give, I may drill down to ask the 'why' behind their style."
> — *Melissa Bixby, Red Shoe Consulting Principal and Founder*

## 2. You Build and Lead Effective Teams

You build solid teams by clearly communicating your leadership style and value proposition. Your team knows what to expect from you and how to work best with you. Team members are then empowered to perform at their highest level. This will help them trust you and make an informed decision about whether your style is a good match for them or not.

"I have a unique hiring method that takes into account both my value proposition and my leadership style. As a communications executive, I see corporate communications skills as a spectrum from one through ten. People close to one are creative idea generators, and people close to ten are operational, results-oriented implementers. A well-functioning communications team has a good balance of people across that spectrum. When I assess my value proposition against that spectrum, I score myself a nine. I'm high on the operational and implementation skills and low on the creative skills. My philosophy when building a team is to balance out my operational strengths by primarily hiring people who score themselves a five or lower on the spectrum. This helps ensure that my team generates continuous, fresh, relevant ideas while I

and a smaller number of efficient operators operationalize and implement them. This method has led me to great success as a F.A.R.E.™ leader: I've been through five acquisitions and have increased brand visibility by over 300 percent in my most recent role."
— *Ally Zwahlen, Vice President, Global Communications, ServiceMax*

### 3. You Lead with Authenticity
Communicate your leadership style so you stay true to it. When you lead authentically, you deliver on your value proposition. Remember, F.A.R.E.™ leaders don't adopt leadership personas to fit in.

"I had never given much thought to whether I was an authentic leader. I was too busy competing, delivering, and trying to fit in. Too often, we focus on trying to be taken seriously or fitting into a mold to meet other people's expectations. I spent too much time figuring out how to get to the next step or role in my career instead of realizing that being authentic would help me be more effective. In hindsight, I realize I adopted personas that I thought would help me fit in and be successful in each role. As it worked, I continued down that path.

"It wasn't until I had many years of experience and quantifiable results behind me and went through the F.A.R.E.™ leadership exercises that I stopped and thought about it. Now that I've identified my leadership style and values, I know who my authentic self is at work. Don't get caught up in trying to fit in. You are you, and you'll make the space for yourself."

— *Chief Investment Officer*

## 4. You Optimize Outcomes

When everyone knows your leadership style, they know how to participate and contribute. This sets clear expectations regarding how to contribute optimally. Each team member maximizes their potential and delivers on their value proposition.

"I co-founded Applaudo Studios—a software development company—in a very crowded space, and we needed to be highly differentiated from every other software development company. I realized that we needed to nurture developers to build up their intuition so they could understand the products and apps they were building and have the confidence to question business requirements and user needs.

"I lead my teams the way I do in order to help them build confidence to assert themselves, be creative, and build up agency so they can actively participate in this process. I see it as investing in their emotional bank accounts and growth progress. Each step in this growth is like a deposit into the account. Examples of doing well, asserting themselves, or acting confidently are deposits. If clients called them out for not having the right answer, it's one withdrawal from that account, not a total drain. This style of leadership enabled us to build up a really strategic and independent team of developers I'm incredibly proud of."
— *Katina Kenyon, Co-founder and former Chief Commercial Officer,*

*Applaudo Studios; Chief Executive Officer, Tree3*

## 5. You Deliver Consistently on Your Value

Your responsibility as a leader is to move the needle. You do that when you deliver on your value proposition and activate your team. Consistent leadership leads to consistent results.

> "A consistent leadership style is important, and it's equally important that your team or stakeholders know what they are getting when they work with you. When you communicate it, your leadership isn't unpredictable or erratic, and neither is your effectiveness. I am as consistent as possible. If you're a good leader, your team should be able to answer the question, 'What would [X] do in this situation?' They know how you would act or respond, and it's a good example for them to embody."
> — *Melissa Waller, President, AIF Global Institute at Alternate Investments Forum*

# 11

# EXAMINE WHY YOU LEAD THE WAY YOU DO

If you think we've finished answering the question, "Who are you as a leader?" I must tell you that we've only covered half of this critical topic. So far, we've answered, "How do you lead?" The second half of the question, "Why do you lead the way that you do?" is a fundamental part of this book and reflects an even more fundamental part of you.

No matter how you lead now or how your leadership style evolves over time, a set of core values forms the foundation of why you lead as you do.

Your leadership values are the reason *why* you lead the way you do. They aren't a set of religious or theological beliefs. Instead, they are connected to your personal belief and value system. They are related to human concepts of relationships, fairness, justice, conflict, and autonomy. When you know your leadership values, you can triangulate important elements of your F.A.R.E.™ leadership. You know how you'll advocate for yourself and your team. You know how you'll bring your value proposition to the table.

When I deliver keynotes or workshops on this topic, the feedback is consistent. Most leaders don't take the time to intentionally think about why they lead the way they do. They don't contemplate what behaviors and situations they will and won't accept from their stakeholders. And they don't prepare themselves for how they'll deal with these inevitable situations.

Here are a few questions to ask yourself as you begin to think about your leadership values:

- What is important to me about my leadership style?
- If I had to give up one aspect of the way I lead, what would I be willing to change, and what would I not budge on? Why?
- What behaviors will I absolutely not accept from my team or my

stakeholders?

- What am I willing to risk in order to stand up for these values?

We're now getting to one of the key reasons I wrote this book and why I'm sharing the F.A.R.E.™ leadership framework with you. To become *fearless, authentic, resilient,* and *effective,* you have to know how you will respond in any situation that challenges your value *or* your values.

If you haven't articulated and internalized your values, it will be much harder to do that.

> "One of my leadership values is that the mission is the most important thing. And, because your people execute that mission, you want to do the best you can to take care of your people. This is the balancing act of leadership: it's broad and strategic, but you can't lose that individual touch. People talk a lot about it but don't do the hard day-to-day leadership work of connecting with people. Taking care of people as a leader is hard work. If you do it right, it takes up 60 percent of your day. But when that is your leadership value, that

is 60 percent of your time well spent, and you focus on it. You make it personal, and you make it deliberate. The higher you get, the harder it becomes, but if this is one of your leadership values, you have to figure out how to personally inject yourself.

"As the commanding officer of the largest communication stations in the navy, I had seventeen sites globally and many thousands of people and their families under my responsibility. I didn't lose touch with people. At least three times a week, I personally made time to walk around the command post and connect with people under my command. If someone was in the hospital or had just had a baby, I would personally visit them. It added an hour to my day three times a week, but it mattered to them, and it mattered to me and is a fundamental part of my leadership values."

— *Danelle Barrett, US Navy Rear Admiral (Retired); Author of Rock the Boat: Embrace Change, Encourage Innovation, and Be a Successful Leader*

The following is an excellent example of how knowing why you lead the way you do can help preserve your value and values.

## Katie's Story

Katie is a creative, pragmatic mother of one, and she is athletic and outdoorsy. She believes in recognizing and promoting talent and mentors the women in her organization. She had been promised a promotion by her manager every year, but the promotion never materialized. Her performance reviews were great, and she and her manager enjoyed a good working relationship.

She came to me to brainstorm ways she could communicate with her manager more effectively on this point and clearly relay why this promotion was so important to her career. She strongly believed that her trajectory at the company should reflect the same message she was conveying to the younger women: if you're doing good work, it will be recognized and rewarded. We agreed that the situation had to change—she had held the same title for nine years, and she was passionate about mentoring and promoting women, yet her requests for a promotion seemed to be falling on uninterested ears.

We created a plan that she presented to her manager. It evidenced her value and requested a formal commitment to promote her. Her manager deferred once again, offering no real reason. Katie was torn. She felt loyal to the women she was mentoring, and she loved the company, but her values were being challenged. She had stood up for herself, advocated, and still nothing changed.

My advice? If you can't change the situation, leave the situation. She interviewed for and secured a role elsewhere that was a full two titles higher. It reflects where she *should* be at this point in her career. She explained to her new organization how important mentorship was to her, and they wrote it into her role. She now officially mentors all the women who are junior to her; far more women than she mentored before.

She is happy with the outcome. She communicated her value, stood up for her values, and then changed the situation when it no longer aligned with her core belief system.

## Challenge 9: Identify Your Leadership Values

# 12

# DECLARE YOUR VALUES AS NON-NEGOTIABLE

I t's easier to internalize your value proposition when you remember that it's an indisputable fact. It's backed up with accomplishments, data, and passion.

The process for internalizing your leadership style and leadership values is similar. Your leadership values are backed up by your core principles. These are what compel you to lead the way you do. They drive you to promote and accept certain behaviors and situations. And when confronted with other behaviors and situations, they alert your intuition that "something isn't right."

Most leaders don't sit down to intentionally articulate, internalize, and communicate their leadership values. They may know *how* they lead, but they haven't identified the underlying principles of *why* they lead that way. These are not F.A.R.E.™ leaders.

When I ask attendees at my keynotes and workshops, "How do you lead?" fewer than one in five has intentionally thought about it and even fewer can actually list and explain their values concisely.

Why is it important to identify this? I've been in situations where I've verbalized my leadership values to explain a decision. If I got pushback, I took the situation off the table. In other words, I walked away to stay in alignment with my values. In writing this book, I want to help leaders like you to also be authentic and fearless about speaking up or stepping away when a situation is misaligned with your core values.

Every day, I hear from women who are in situations that test their leadership values. Instead of communicating those values or walking away, they remain silent. They betray their authentic leadership style. They become less resilient as they battle their way through these situations. And they become less effective.

How do you handle these situations as a F.A.R.E.™ leader? I offer the following three distinct ways:

1) **Identify your leadership values.** Know why you lead the way you do.

2) **Internalize your leadership values.** Your leadership values are indisputable principles. They are not opinions you need to defend. They are a sacred framework and commitment you've made to yourself and to your team. They are a critical foundation of your F.A.R.E.™ leadership.

3) **Communicate your leadership values.** In a difficult situation, explain why you are deciding or choosing to act in a specific way. You are staying true to your leadership values, which are non-negotiable.

Remembering this will help you handle situations that challenge your leadership values, and it will keep you consistent as a leader.

Here's what two F.A.R.E.™ leaders have to say about having and affirming their non-negotiable values:

"There are two non-negotiables in my leadership. 1) I won't ask anyone to do anything I wouldn't do myself. As a leader, I'm the frontline defense for my team, so I take the heat for any decision. 2) I don't take credit for anything anyone on my team does. My responsibility is to lift them up, so they have the autonomy to grow their careers and get the credit when they succeed."
— *CEO*

———————//———————

"When meeting the executive team in person for the first time during my onboarding, we had an opportunity to share about what made each of us who we are today as leaders. Tissa and I had prepared for this in our work together, so I had a ready answer about my leadership values: courage, curiosity, and integrity. Having these values at my fingertips and being ready to talk about them made the session more valuable and helped me get to know my fellow leaders much quicker."

— *Lerk-Ling Chang, Chief Strategy Officer, FinalSite*

Remember that contemplating your non-negotiable leadership values in advance enables you to respond to all challenges, including the most complex ones, with a sense of preparedness and assurance because you already know where you stand on the essentials. Taking the time to intentionally contemplate the lines you won't cross over can prevent you from making a regrettable decision under pressure.

TRY IT YOURSELF!

**Challenge 10: Internalize Your Values**

# 13

# PRACTICE YOUR VALUES

As a F.A.R.E.™ leader, you will find yourself stepping up to advocate for yourself and your team in all situations that warrant it. When your team members know you have their backs, they'll operate at maximum effectiveness.

You'll be comfortable and confident handling these situations within the F.A.R.E.™ leadership framework. You will deliver on your catalyst statement. You will lead your team a certain way, and you will lead that way because of your values. Moreover, you will communicate those values to remind your stakeholders of what you stand for and why you are standing up for it.

One of the most popular topics for my keynotes is leadership brand and values. In every company I founded and led, a consistent goal was to create and maintain a culture of calm respect. This manifests in a leadership culture of no yelling, raised voices, or interpersonal disrespect. A calm, supportive workplace culture is critical to activating my F.A.R.E.™ leadership. This is especially important in the fast-paced, highly stressful environment of early-stage startups.

My leadership is authentic to my values. I walk away from situations or opportunities that don't align with this tenet. I present my leadership values as the reason I'm stepping back from the situation or taking it off the table. As a founder and CEO, I've disengaged from potential customers or investors who are disrespectful. I prioritize a supportive, peaceful environment for my teams over one more deal or investment.

Several years ago, my software engineers were on a call with a prospective acquirer. It was immediately clear that the other team operated under a completely different leadership style and held divergent values. The tone was aggressive. The other engineers interrupted my team nonstop and were difficult to interact with. Despite the potential damage to the deal, I didn't hesitate to respectfully let the other company know we would end the call. I explained that our cultures were orthogonal, and we wouldn't align. My team had worked around the clock for years to build a company with me, and I stood up for them. I stay authentic to my leadership principles: respect for my team.

Another leadership value is to always focus on ethics. If a situation feels even slightly ambiguous, I walk away. In the past, making the decision to walk away has cost me and my family millions of dollars. While financially painful, I have no regrets about the decision. In fact, being mindful of ethics turned what could have been a difficult choice into the obvious and only possibility.

I stay aligned with and authentic to my leadership values at all times, even if it means taking entire situations off the table. I don't defend my values; I present them factually. I do it without fear, and I do it with resilience and confidence. When you take the time to define your leadership values, you will handle similar situations in the same way. That's a key part of F.A.R.E.™ leadership.

If I asked you, "What kind of leader are you?" the answer should automatically be, "One with clear, non-negotiable leadership values." The following stories show you what it looks like when leaders have internalized their values so it becomes automatic to respond to situations in a values-oriented way.

———— // ————

"Several years ago, I was in a role where the culture was not aligned with my leadership style and values. I didn't leave the role quickly enough because I was focused on two things: I was fighting for my team, and I thought if I kept getting promoted, I could change the culture from higher up. Those reasons weren't sufficient. My team knew I was fighting for them, but I couldn't turn an aircraft carrier around by myself, and my energy and resilience were depleted. Even if I'd been promoted, the organizational culture was too different from my values for me to make wholesale changes.

"Finally, I decided to leave. When I left, several of my team asked what took so long. They've been supportive of my decision. In hindsight, I should have left much earlier, but I hesitated

because there was some fear. I hadn't sufficiently internalized my value proposition. The job was a comfort zone, even though it wasn't a good fit. I learned I had to trust that I would land in the right place if I was intentional and communicated my value. I will choose more carefully next time and not stay in a mismatch for as long."
— *Chief Operating Officer*

———————//———————

"My story is one of finding the courage to exit a situation that did not align with my operating principles and where I was not able to demonstrate my value proposition. A few years ago, I was an executive at a corporate-sponsored startup subsidiary. With the rest of the executive team, I worked tirelessly to develop a growth strategy, a company value proposition, and our various product platforms. We were successful, and clients were happy. However, our corporate owner was facing expense pressure and wanted to see faster growth from us. Their solution was to merge three similar businesses. My new role was to combine three product offerings into a single one, addressing a broad client market that varied in terms of needs and service. The newly formed executive team had been forced together in the merger, and it was an uphill battle from the start. Finding cohesiveness and focus as a team was difficult. We had aggressive growth targets and a lot of chefs—and egos—in the kitchen. It got harder and harder to do my job identifying synergies and driving aggressive growth.

"This made me question my abilities and skills and everything I'd brought to the table so far. It took introspection to realize that the problem wasn't *me*. It was just not the right environment to demonstrate my value proposition. It took a lot of sleepless nights to finally come to the conclusion that, despite the high-paying, prestigious role, it was time for me to leave. I felt really good after my decision—as if a huge weight had been lifted.

"I share this story to communicate that one experience shouldn't make you question your self-worth or your abilities. The environment or the timing can present too many opposing forces for you to act on your value proposition. Those are the times you need to remind yourself of your strengths, accomplishments, value proposition, and operating principles. Stick to them and create your own fate."
— *Chief Financial Officer*

———*//*———

"I spent two years negotiating one of the biggest deals in our company's history and earned a large commission. Unfortunately, the customer defaulted on the contract. Because the company had a larger, long-term engagement with the customer, a business decision was made not to try to collect on the defaulted contract. In turn, the company told me it would be clawing back the commission that had been paid out to me a full year prior. My performance—and compensation—

related to closing the deal should not have been impacted by the company's business decision not to collect on the contract. While I agreed with the company's decision from a customer relationship perspective, leadership should never penalize employees who do their job right. The contract was bulletproof (for example, there was no term for convenience). I did everything right. Choosing to claw back a commission set a dangerous precedent for the broader organization, as every seller now realized they could do everything right and still not be paid. The company made an unethical decision to punish a top performer who had dotted every "i" and crossed every "t." I told the executive staff that if this was their final decision, I would choose to resign. I couldn't work for a company that made unethical choices like that. It took the company one day to decide not to claw back my commission after all. For me, it was about the principle and ethics and not about the money."

— *Chief Revenue Officer*

"In a financial crisis, the management team had decided to only pay bonuses to senior executives and not to pay bonuses to employees. That didn't sit well with me. You're either a leader of one or a leader of all. I didn't hesitate. I announced to management that I would forfeit my bonus and requested that it instead be distributed to my team. At the core of my decision was the underlying principle that the goals those bonuses were paid out on were achieved by teams, not by individuals. I'm not a leader of one; I'm a leader of my team."

**— Senior Banking Industry Executive**

"I'm very protective of my team. Every leader should be thinking about their people because they're what makes an organization tick. In an annual planning meeting several years ago, I noticed that someone had introduced an accelerator and a de-accelerator proposal for my sales team. (Sales accelerators give account executives more commission once they hit 100 percent of their target. De-accelerators are the inverse. If an account executive only hits 50 percent of their target, for example, they may receive no variable payout at all.) The de-accelerator seemed like it would be demoralizing for my team. It also felt like the organization was trying to use it as a performance management tool to phase people out. There are better ways to manage people without leveraging compensation. It wasn't the right decision for the existing team, and that kind of compensation plan would have made it difficult to acquire rockstar sales talent going forward. I advocated for my team and pushed back hard against it, and the executive team agreed. These are the kinds of things you have to be constantly aware of and advocating for as a leader."

— *Laura Zwahlen, Chief Revenue Officer*

---

"As the CEO, I have to make difficult decisions based on what's best for the company, my team, and my values. A key value is getting results. We had someone who was really good at his job and who I cared about personally and professionally. But he hated rules. Some rules we have to follow legally and some I ask the company to follow for efficiency and so we can deliver value for our customers.

"This person violated the rules we are legally bound by and refused to comply with company guidelines. I tried all of the tricks I knew to make it work. But it became a legal liability, and I saw it was creating conflict and chaos with the rest of my team. He was very effective within the narrower confines of his job, but at some point, the balance of pain to gain wasn't viable anymore.

"Our values were divergent, and it wasn't good for my energy and effectiveness as a CEO and leader to be constantly mediating the conflict he created. Despite our best efforts, it became clear that we couldn't overcome our differences in values. I asked him to

leave the company. When you have a set of values you lead by, you have to put those first, or your team won't continue to believe in or trust you."
— *Melynda Caudle, CEO, Cooper Consulting*

———— // ————

Have you thought about how you practice your values lately? It is a wonderful exercise in determining whether you are being as authentic a leader as you could be.

TRY IT YOURSELF!

Challenge 11: Practice Values-Based Leadership

PART THREE

# YOUR LIFE

# 14

# LIVE AS A LEADER

You've done the work of becoming a F.A.R.E.™ leader. You know who you are and the value you bring. You also know who you are as a leader, how you lead, and why.

Equipped with this knowledge, you've unlocked your leadership potential. Now it's time to consider how you will handle situations in work that have broader implications for your life—the ones that challenge your values or that make you uneasy. It's time to answer the question, "Who are you in your life?"

As a leader, you will face challenging or uncomfortable situations. Some are inevitable parts of leadership. Some situations don't "feel right." Some go beyond being uncomfortable and make you question whether you should speak up and take action. How will you make decisions and handle such situations in a fearless, authentic, resilient, and effective way?

I'm sure you've been in at least some of these situations:

- Being the lone dissenting voice on an important issue.
- Dealing with or dreading conflict.
- Being in a job or organization you don't enjoy anymore.
- Dealing with a bullying or abrasive personality.
- Recognizing that the culture of your organization isn't functioning effectively.
- Deciding how to handle unfair or unethical situations or behaviors.

Let's break down the F.A.R.E.™ leadership framework and see how you'll handle situations like these once you're equipped with the knowledge of your value and your values.

I intentionally chose the acronym "F.A.R.E.™" for this framework. The words *fearless, authentic, resilient, and effective* appear in that sequence because when you are fearless, you can be your authentic self. When you are fearless and authentic, you are resilient. And when you are fearless, authentic, and resilient, you are your most effective.

## *FEARLESS*

Fear constricts vision and thought. Fear is driven by the worry that you don't have the operational or moral authority to speak up or that your value or credibility isn't recognized. It's magnified by the concern that your decisions or actions will be fatal to the situation or your career.

When you internalize your value and your values, you operate with an eye for the longer term. When situations don't align with your leadership values, you don't fear speaking up. You know that few situations are irrecoverable. This specific customer deal, investment opportunity, or job may not materialize. But you know there will be others. Speaking up or walking away is more authentic to your values than doing nothing.

As a F.A.R.E.™ leader, you learn to handle fear with greater comfort. You displace fear with the knowledge of your value and your values. You know your value and credibility are recognized because you present them factually. You become comfortable speaking up.

## *AUTHENTIC*

Fearlessness drives authenticity. As a F.A.R.E.™ leader, you are comfortable advocating for your value and your values. Without fear, you are authentic. You create the space to operate genuinely and evoke trust with your stakeholders. As a F.A.R.E.™ leader, you don't adopt a persona to fit in or be liked. You show up and present your value as a fact and your values as non-negotiable principles. You have a demonstrable track record and confidence in the *way* you lead and *why* you lead that way.

Authenticity means you are recognizably *you*. People will know how you're likely to respond or react, providing the consistency and reliability necessary for effective leadership. You'll develop a reputation for delivering on your value proposition. You'll be known for your principles and trusted to make the right decisions.

## RESILIENT

Fearlessness and authenticity drive resilience. Resilience is the ability to develop a consistent, adaptable, flexible response to challenges. As a F.A.R.E.™ leader, you aren't thrown off by difficult situations. You are comfortable taking options off the table and advocating for your values. You develop a thoughtful, consistent response to challenging situations. Most importantly, you handle difficulties with calmness.

Resilience is important to you *and* your leadership. When your resilience is impacted, everything is impacted—your stress levels, your health, your sleep, and your family life. The ability to handle situations calmly and with confidence leaves you with more energy for all other parts of leadership and life. You can make any decision—a high-stakes or low-stakes decision—with clarity and with energy left over for both work and life.

## EFFECTIVE

When you are fearless, authentic, and resilient, you are the most effective leader possible. You deliver on the promise of your value proposition. You advocate and stand up for your leadership style and your leadership values. You get the best work possible out of your team and yourself. You know your value, and so does everyone around you. You have nothing to defend and nothing to doubt. You operate from a place of calmness, confidence, and purpose. You know who you are. You know who you are as a leader, and you know who you are in your life. You are a F.A.R.E.™ leader.

# 15

# TAKE THE ULTIMATE CHALLENGE

It's easy to become super busy while being a leader. You get caught up in the momentum. You're engaged in delivering on your value proposition, guiding teams, and executing on your leadership potential. For all these reasons and more, it's also easy to forget the important work we've done together in this book.

A way to not forget the important work is to challenge yourself to live your leadership daily …

Print out your catalyst statement, leadership style, and leadership values. Put them above your desk where you will see them every day.

When they are right in front of you in black and white, you will be regularly reminded of your value and your values. Your F.A.R.E.™ leadership is stronger when you see the framework it's built upon every single day.

> "Unless you write your catalyst statement down and reference it daily, it can be easy for it not to stick. You forget it, or you lose it as you get busy with the day-to-day of delivering on it. If you've done the work to whittle it down to one sentence, put it in front of you. Print it out, along with your values, to remind you to live them every day. It's more impactful that way."
> — *Eryn Logan, Senior Marketing Manager, Charles Schwab*

Here are the statements I want you to complete and print:

- **My Catalyst Statement:** *I bring the following value …*
- **My Leadership Style:** *I lead the following way …*
- **My Leadership Values:** *I lead that way because …*

By way of example, here is what I have printed above my desk:

- I help leaders develop an unshakable sense of self so they can perform at their peak and lead values-based, high-performing teams.
- I lead with empathy, curiosity, and transparency.
- I lead that way because I value respect, honesty, and ethics.

Having a visual reminder of the hard work you've done is powerful. You've taken the time to identify and articulate your value and your values. Don't put them in a drawer and forget about them. You can't reach your full F.A.R.E.™ leadership potential that way. Put them front and center so you can internalize, communicate, and live them every day.

"Most executives have leaders that have inspired them, and they may keep reminders of those leaders around them. In the military, many of those inspirational leaders are great military figures. On my wall at the Pentagon, I had a poster of Walt Disney. It may have been the only poster of Disney at the Pentagon.

"I had the poster up to remind me of why I lead the way I do. Disney was a leader who wasn't afraid to fail. He took risks and chances and had big, creative, innovative vision. He was a creative agent of transformation. Anyone who can look at a swamp in Florida and envision thousands of acres of spinning teacups and flying elephants is a visionary. He also translated his bold ideas into reality. That is a true visionary leader. Disney also knew his limitations and got the smart people around him to do the things he couldn't do. For example, he wasn't the businessman in the Disney equation— he left that to his brother Roy.

"That's the kind of leader I modeled myself after, and keeping that poster up reminded me daily to live those values."
— *Danelle Barrett, US Navy Rear Admiral (Retired); Author of Rock the Boat: Embrace Change, Encourage Innovation, and Be a Successful Leader*

## TRY IT YOURSELF!

# 16

# KNOW YOU WILL F.A.R.E.™ WELL

## CONGRATULATIONS!

You've completed your journey through the F.A.R.E.™ leadership framework and challenges. You understand why it's so critical to know your value, your leadership style, and your values. You now have the tools to operate at your highest potential.

You are:

- **FEARLESS:** You stand up for yourself, your team, your value, and your values.
- **AUTHENTIC:** You lead your team optimally, maximizing their success and yours.
- **RESILIENT:** You are strong and adaptable in the face of any challenge or situation.

- **EFFECTIVE:** You deliver consistently on your value proposition.

You know the answers to the questions:

- Who are you?
- Who are you as a leader?
- Who are you in your life?

You have never needed anyone's permission to lead the way you do. It's been inside you all along, part of your leadership DNA. It's a natural, authentic part of your character that you express in every decision you make and in every situation you respond to.

This book simply prompted you to think intentionally about how you lead and why you lead that way. It guided you to unlock your leadership potential so you can succeed and thrive.

Congratulations and FAREwell, F.A.R.E.™ leader. Go do great things. Leave your leadership legacy.

# PART FOUR
# CHALLENGES

## Challenge 1: Create Your Value Proposition

When completing these challenges, I encourage you to literally put pen to paper. I always suggest that my executive coaching clients do this. It shakes up your cognitive flow and encourages you to get out of the habit of staring at a screen or device all day. We spend 90 percent of the work week typing on a variety of devices, so looking at a different surface is good for your brain. You can check out my website for more details about why and how I encourage you to give this old-fashioned method a try.

I also want you to be in the right frame of mind when you approach these F.A.R.E.™ leadership challenges. You're taking the initiative to be intentional and invest in yourself. Find quiet time. Pour yourself a glass of wine, coffee, or tea. Choose a place where you don't usually work. Sit in a comfortable chair or couch or even somewhere peaceful outdoors. You're about to dive deep into the value you bring to the table, and I want you to be able to focus on that.

## QUESTION 1

Make a list of the major accomplishments, skills, and outcomes of your career so far. If you would include it on a resume or talk about it in a job interview, list it here.

## QUESTION 2

Remember the reporter questions? We'll use some of them as "starters" here. Ask yourself the following questions about each item on the list. Include as many metrics as you can for each question.

What challenge, problem, or need was I addressing?

How did I analyze and approach the situation?

What skills were required to solve the challenge, problem, or need?

What was the outcome?

How did I deliver the outcome?

Who benefited, and how?

**Note:**

Your value proposition is the most data-driven of the F.A.R.E.™ leadership challenges you'll complete in this book. Bring in as many hard numbers as you can. Be specific. What was the budget for a project? What revenue gains resulted? How many people did you manage? How much money did you raise? What growth percentage did you drive? Include as much detail as you can. You'll use this data to back up your value proposition when you communicate it to stakeholders.

If your role doesn't lend itself to quantitative analysis, don't worry. You've contributed value that led to quantitative results. I encourage you to keep track of numbers wherever possible. Have you started a new marketing or brand campaign? Have you initiated a shareholder communications program? Have you launched any initiative relevant to your value proposition? Get close to the data teams at your organization. Ask them to help you identify and analyze data that shows how your work is driving value.

Believe me: You are delivering value. If you weren't, you wouldn't have landed and stayed in your current position (or any position).

## QUESTION 3

Now we'll group the brainstorming you've done *in this section* into three primary areas, based on the following questions: Who do you help? How do you help them? Why does it matter? (The latter being the "*So what?*" question.)

*Who* do you help?

- Who are your stakeholders?
- What are they struggling with or trying to accomplish?

*How* do you help them?

- What do you do that solves their problem or challenge?
- What have you done over and over that makes you valuable to the people or organizations that you help?

*So what?*

- Why does what you do matter?
- What is the outcome when you deliver your value?
- What problems do you solve?
- What blockers do you remove?

- What growth do you enable?
- How do you drive change or transformation?
- Why do people care about your results? (So what?)

Use the following space to answer these questions.

*Who* have I helped?

*How* have I helped them?

*Why* does it matter? (So what?)

## QUESTION 4
Themes should appear. You help a common set of stakeholders (*who*). You have helped them address a common set of challenges by solving those challenges in a consistent way (*how*). And, those outcomes matter in a consistent way (*so what*).

What themes are appearing?

## QUESTION 5
Write down the final "who, how, and so what" results. You may have more than one result for

each of these categories. That's okay. Write them all down.

I help who

I help them how

So what

## QUESTION 6
Use the F.A.R.E.™ formula to create a draft of your value proposition sentence. Focus on the SO WHAT.

The following is an example:

> When Sophie and I worked on her value proposition exercise, she kept pointing to her pattern of leading massive digital transformation initiatives for large enterprises. I asked her to think about whether that was really the highest value (or the highest "so what") of her work. Why were those organizations asking her to lead those digital transformation projects? What benefits did they bring? What was the digital transformation in service to?
>
> Her answer? "Moving things to the cloud brings a lot of efficiency and

security, speeds up software development, eliminates redundancies, and enables the organization to divert those costs to developing more innovative products and capabilities." **AHA! That's the *so what*.**

So, here's an example of how she could word that as a value proposition statement:

I maximize profitability and innovation for large enterprises by increasing efficiency and security through digital transformation initiatives.

Use the following sentence structure to practice your value proposition:

*I do [so what] for [who] by [how].*

It's okay if your sentence follows a different sequence. Let's look at Kathleen's value proposition. It's structured as: Kathleen helps [who], [so what], by [how].

- Kathleen is a CxO who helps *[who:] public SaaS companies*
- to *[so what:] increase recurring revenue, enlarge market share, and*

*create operational efficiencies*

- by *[how:] optimizing customer experiences to delight customers*

The most important idea is that the information is there, and it makes sense when people read or hear it.

Give it a try. It may not be beautiful on your first few attempts. That's what we are here to work on together!

**Note:**
You'll want to revisit your value proposition several times to see if it accurately identifies who you bring value to, how you do it, and why it matters (so what). Don't worry about wordsmithing it into a perfect, final sentence or catchy phrase right now.

Your value proposition will evolve as you share it with people and get feedback. Ask your mentors and trusted peers if you've captured a value proposition you've delivered on previously. Practice communicating it. Edit and work with it until it feels right to you.

You might notice that your value proposition is longer than one sentence. As you iterate yours, you may need one to three sentences to communicate your value. That's fine. Convey the who, how, and so what as succinctly and compellingly as possible. What's more important— conveying your value effectively or cramming it into a single sentence?

I'll let you in on a secret. I do this professionally, yet as I was writing this book, I was still iterating my value proposition. I've shared a previous version with many thousands of people in keynotes, workshops, and online courses, and it was fine, but I couldn't help revisiting and refining it here once again. It's a living statement. Mine will keep evolving, and so will yours. So, don't worry about whether it's perfectly worded. Instead, focus on ensuring that it accurately reflects the value you bring right now. Just go ahead and try it.

Here's a bonus you'll derive from doing the four-step exercise in this chapter: It will help you refine your resume, bio, and LinkedIn profile. It will also help you present your accomplishments succinctly during interviews and networking opportunities.

_Continue with Chapter 3_.

## Challenge 2: Align Your Passion with Your Value Proposition

**QUESTION 1**
Look at the value proposition you wrote down in Question 6 of the previous exercise. We want to make sure it is aligned with your passions so that your work brings you as much joy as possible. Here are honest questions to ask yourself to help you do that.

What energizes you?

What makes you excited to work on a project or initiative?

When you look at a job description, what tasks would you cross off and hope never to have to do again?

If you created your ideal role, what would it look like, and why?

Which of your accomplishments best align with your personal values, your mission, and your most fulfilling work?

Describe your value proposition and your accomplishments to someone else. When and where in the description do you become animated and happy? Take note of those places. They reveal a lot.

This is not a soft or squishy undertaking. If you don't properly align your passion and your value, you risk doing work that doesn't fulfill you or make you happy. As a F.A.R.E.™ leader, you will be less resilient, less authentic, and far less effective. In short: you won't truly be you.

When someone asks, "Who are you?" you can now answer with both your value and your passions— a powerful combination.

*Continue with Chapter 4*.

## Challenge 3: Create Your Catalyst Statement

It's time to take your value proposition and evolve it into a powerful catalyst statement.

**QUESTION 1**
Write down the value proposition draft statement you finished in Question 6 of Challenge 1.
Read your draft statement with an unbiased eye. Does it truly convey the *so what* part of the answer to the "Who are you?" question? Is it at all generic? Does it focus too much on *what you do* instead of *why it matters*? Is it a catalyst statement yet?

**QUESTION 2**
Remember, the purpose of a catalyst statement is to crystallize:

- How people understand you
- How people remember you
- How people take action in response to you

Brainstorming the following will help you realign your value proposition with your catalyzers.

I want people to immediately understand the following …

> Example: That I am skilled at translating the business value of complex technologies so that CxOs understand them and shorten the buying cycle.

> Example: That I reduce risk in global e-commerce platforms so customers trust them more rapidly, enabling them to scale and hit revenue targets.

1) I want people to immediately understand …

2) I want people to immediately understand …

3) I want people to immediately understand …

I want people to remember …

> Example: I want people to remember me when they need a CEO for a fast-

growing technology startup that needs to raise money.

Example: I want people to remember that I'm a brand evangelist and can make any brand recognizable and loved.

1) I want people to remember ...

2) I want people to remember ...

3) I want people to remember ...

After meeting me, I want people to ...

Example: After meeting me, I want people to think of me when they need a CTO for a public CPG company.

Example: After meeting me, I want people to suggest me as a speaker and corporate trainer for their company.

1) After meeting me, I want people to ...

2) After meeting me, I want people to ...

3) After meeting me, I want people to ...

**QUESTION 3**

Now let's revisit your catalyst statement. How can you make it more impactful, specific, and catalyzing? Brainstorm a few revisions below.

## QUESTION 4
How did this exercise feel? Have you thought about these questions before? Does it make you uncomfortable to be so intentional about how you want to be perceived, understood, and remembered? Why do you think that is?

*Continue with Chapter 5*.

# Challenge 4: Internalize Your Value

As you've seen from the stories so far, internalizing your value is transformational. It gives you the courage to start companies, shut them down (as I once did), control your narrative, negotiate for compensation, land your dream job, and much more. When you embody your value, you set the foundation for the rest of your journey to becoming a F.A.R.E.™ leader.

In this challenge, I want you to embrace and internalize your value.

If you've accurately identified your catalyst statement, it should resonate with you. (If it doesn't, iterate a bit more.) Practice saying it aloud. I suggest having a conversation with yourself in your car or shower. My shower has heard from me on a wide variety of topics! These are safe, nonjudgmental places to grow in confidence while factually, calmly, and comfortably talking about your value.

I want you to say things like "I am …," "I do …," and "It matters because …" as easily and as matter-of-factly as you would if you were telling someone that Tuesday at 2 p.m. works best for your next meeting. Practice doing this as often as necessary.

List three "I am ..." statements:

Example: I am an executive director who connects investors with founders so they can scale their companies rapidly.

1) I am ...

2) I am ...

3) I am ...

List three "I do ..." statements:

Example: I do this by understanding the investment theses of investors and the unique business models of startups, and making thoughtful, high-quality introductions.

1) I do ...

2) I do ...

3) I do ...

List three "So what ..." statements:

Example: I've helped over a dozen young startups get critical funding, be acquired, or scale to hypergrowth because of this.

1) So what?

2) So what?

3) So what?

Take the time to re-read, internalize, and celebrate what you've written. Remember, these statements are factual.

Congratulations!

*Continue with Chapter 6*.

# Challenge 5: Communicate Your Value

It's important to practice delivering your catalyst statement verbally in as many situations as possible, including networking events, interviews, performance reviews, and everyday conversations.

Adapt it for the situation. Explain why you do what you do, the *so what* of your value, and why you are explaining it to your audience. For example, let your team know so they are inspired by your credibility, or let your network know so they can introduce you to appropriate contacts.

Practice including your catalyst statement in conversations or situations where it is additive. (Hint: It's almost always additive.)

Also practice saying things like "I don't bring value in that situation" when you are asked to do an activity that is misaligned with your catalyst statement.

Get comfortable presenting your value as a fact. Feel yourself becoming more at ease saying it. Notice how it starts to feel natural. Observe how it no longer feels arrogant but instead feels contextual and purposeful. Notice how it feels like *you*.

For this challenge, identify an upcoming situation where communicating your value will optimize the outcome. Do you need to advocate for a promotion or a raise? Do you need to have a discussion with a member of your team about their performance or lack thereof?

Write down talking points for the conversation. Include your catalyst statement and why the value you bring matters. Practice it. Have the conversation, then write down how you felt and why communicating your value made a difference.

What is the situation?

How will communicating your value make a difference?

What are your key talking points?

How did it feel to include your catalyst statement in the conversation?

*Continue with Part Two*.

# Challenge 6: Identify Your Leadership Style

We're ready to find out how you lead. It's important to convey your style to your team and stakeholders. It's a critical part of F.A.R.E.™ leadership, so prepare to articulate your philosophy. Let's get started.

**QUESTION 1**
Think about leaders who have inspired you. What was inspirational, and how did it manifest in their leadership?

**QUESTION 2**
How has your leadership been described? (You've likely taken leadership or personality assessments, or your leadership style has been described in your performance reviews. If possible, find those previous results or descriptions. If you don't have them, don't stress. Ask trusted team members or managers to describe your leadership to you in a few words.)

Which descriptions resonate with you and feel authentic? Which descriptions align most closely with you when you are activating your value?

## QUESTION 3
Look for emerging themes. By now, you might have words that look as if they came from a thesaurus. Group similar words from your previous lists so we can start to narrow down those themes.

## QUESTION 4
Shorten the list of words in each group so they only include those that feel right to you. Aim for three to five words total.

For example, if "sensitive" and "empathetic" keep appearing, include only the one that is more authentic. Being sensitive may be how you *manifest* your empathetic leadership style.

Or, if "supportive" and "collaborative" keep appearing, figure out which one feels more apt. Again, one of them (being supportive) may be how you *manifest* your collaborative leadership style.

## QUESTION 5
Create three to five bullet points that explain how your leadership style manifests in practice.

Here's an example of what the output from Question 5 would look like using my leadership style:

I lead with empathy, curiosity, and transparency.
*How does that manifest? What can my team expect?*

- They will have the freedom and safety to experiment.
- They will have a workplace free of disrespect.
- They will always have the information they need to make the right decisions.
- They know I will advocate for them and put their well-being first, no matter what situation that puts me in as a leader.

I lead with ...

How does this manifest? My team can expect ...

Here's how this looks in practice as a startup founder and CEO:

My leadership style and my personal brand are closely related. My brand is bold, trusted, and authentic. And I lead with empathy, curiosity, and transparency. I speak up for my team and foster a culture of experimentation, which is critical in a startup. I create a safe environment where my team can be open and curious and try new things without fear of failure. The engineers at my last company suggested that we port our software to a new operating system. They felt it would make our product more robust, competitive, and future-proof. The decision was costly, time-consuming, and delayed customer implementations. But they felt safe suggesting and trying it, and they had a compelling set of reasons. Ultimately, it was the right choice for our company.

Even if it had been the wrong choice, no one would have been punished. As a F.A.R.E.™ leader, I'm authentic to my leadership style. My teams know I support curiosity and experimentation. After all, that's how startups become successful.

# Challenge 7: Commit to Your Leadership Style

With this particular challenge, I invite you to do more than *try it*—I encourage you to *be it*. The call to action is to internalize your leadership style. It should feel authentic and natural to you. It should be easy and comfortable for you to tell people about how you lead.

In this case, internalizing your leadership style is about truly integrating it in all the ways you work. It's easy to *talk* about leading with empathy or collaboration—but are you truly manifesting that style in everything you do? Is there alignment between how you think you lead (or want to lead) and how you lead in practice?

Leadership is complicated. There are a lot of elements involved. It may take a while for you to integrate your aspirational leadership style with your actual twenty-four-seven leadership style. That's okay. The purpose of this challenge is to get you thinking about it and to get you started.

Think about the challenge we just completed. It's important to know and believe in your leadership style. Without looking back at your previous challenge, answer the following questions. Then compare them to the results from the earlier challenge!

How do you lead?

How does that leadership style manifest?

What can your team expect from you?

*Continue with Chapter 9*.

## Challenge 8: Communicate Your Leadership Style

When did you last communicate your leadership style to your team—or to anyone?

It's important to take the time to explain how you lead and how that creates results for you, your team, and your organization.

The next time you interview new talent, conduct a performance review, or interview for a new role for yourself, take the time to explain how you lead and how that activates your value proposition.

Whether you are hiring talent or interviewing for your own new role, you'll be asked about your leadership style. Be ready to talk honestly and authentically about the exercise we just did.

In this challenge, imagine you are interviewing for a new leadership role. (Perhaps you are actually interviewing for a role right now!) Write down how you lead, why it matters, and an example. This allows for a much more robust answer to the question, "Tell me about your leadership style."

What is your leadership style?

How does that leadership style secure results from you and your team?

What is an example of how practicing this leadership style secured positive results?

*Continue with Chapter 11*.

# Challenge 9: Identify Your Leadership Values

It's exciting to intentionally identify your leadership values. It's a huge part of the F.A.R.E.™ leadership framework. Few leaders take the time to think about this important topic, so congratulations! In the next three questions, you will articulate the reasons you lead the way you do. This makes it easier to handle challenging situations with resilience.

*This exercise is easier to follow if you have an example as a reference. I'll illustrate it with my leadership style and leadership values.*

## QUESTION 1
Write down your leadership style and explain why it's important to you.

The following is an example:

I lead with empathy, curiosity, and transparency.
*Why is this important to me?*

- Because I respect people
- Because everyone deserves compassion

- Because the truth is critical to me
- Because honest, ethical behavior is more important to me than money or success
- Because I want to understand why people do what they do
- Because I want to know what is possible

I lead with ...

This is important to me because ...

## QUESTION 2

Now, identify your leadership "non-negotiables." This helps you define what you'll stand up against when a situation or behavior is not aligned with your values. As a F.A.R.E.™ leader, you'll have the confidence and courage to advocate for this set of non-negotiables.

Here's an example using mine.

My non-negotiables are:

- Yelling or disrespect
- Lying or dishonesty
- Unethical conduct

My leadership non-negotiables are ...

**QUESTION 3**

When your list of leadership non-negotiables is complete, identify the opposite of those. That's how you'll surface your leadership values! I love this step because you've already defined your values without realizing it. Your values are the opposites of your non-negotiables. They are the core principles you won't give up under any circumstances.

Here's an example using my non-negotiables and values:

Tissa's Non-Negotiables

1. Yelling or disrespect

2. Lying or dishonesty

3. Unethical conduct

Tissa's Leadership Values

1. Respect

2. Honesty

3. Ethics

My leadership values are respect, honesty, and ethics.

What are yours?

My Non-Negotiables (from Question 2)

My Leadership Values (from Question 2)

Your leadership values don't have to be one-word descriptors. If you need to use short phrases to capture them accurately, that's fine. It's more important that they reflect the precise principles underlying the way you lead and that they clearly state what you will advocate for.

*Continue with Chapter 12.*

# Challenge 10: Internalize Your Values

Internalizing your leadership values is absolutely essential to becoming a F.A.R.E.™ leader and handling any situation. Can you visualize your leadership values right now in your mind? Can you tell someone about them and explain why they are non-negotiable to you?

In this challenge, we'll work through an actual situation and apply your leadership values to it.

**Describe a situation in which having your values clearly defined would have helped you be more fearless, authentic, resilient, and effective.**

**How would you have handled the situation differently today?**

Visualize how you'll activate these values as a leader going forward. Say your values out loud to yourself. Explain *why* they are non-negotiable and fundamental to you. Get comfortable explaining them as facts.

*Continue with Chapter 13*.

# Challenge 11: Practice Values-Based Leadership

As a values-based F.A.R.E.™ leader, you need to be consistent and approach situations through the lens of your values. Leadership is a muscle. Practice while the stakes are small so the big-stakes situations won't throw you. Is a situation making you uneasy? Is it misaligned with your values? To be a values-based leader, you will have to get comfortable expressing your values and noting which are driving your decisions, and why.

As you practice, you will start to react automatically, always advocating for your values, no matter the cost.

Keep your values at the forefront of your mind so that speaking up about and acting on them will come naturally to you. This will pay off in your leadership and your life.

In this challenge, we'll explore a situation through the lens of your values, looking at how you might have handled it before becoming a F.A.R.E.™ leader versus how you would handle it now.

Identify a situation in your life or work that you need to address.

What about this situation is misaligned with your values?

How would you have handled this situation before becoming a F.A.R.E.™ leader? Or how have you been dealing with it until now?

Next, approach this situation from the perspective of your non-negotiable leadership values. What needs to change? Can you start a conversation about it by leading with your values? Don't defend them; they are facts. Do you need to take the situation off the table or exit the situation?

How did you feel before you approached this situation as a values-based F.A.R.E.™ leader? How do you feel now? How did people react when you explained your values?

*Continue with Part Three*.

# Challenge 12: State Your Leadership Values as Facts

You are a F.A.R.E.™ leader now. You know how to handle a variety of situations. You know to never defend your value, your leadership, or your values because they are facts. To ensure that you always state your values without defense, you must be comfortable with phrases that internalize and communicate your value and your values.

This final challenge provides you with practice expressing your leadership values as facts so you are prepared to do so in different situations.

Complete the sentences below: "I bring the greatest value when I …"

This can be focused on the value you bring or the values that guide you.

> Example: I bring the greatest value when I commercialize new products for fast-growing healthcare companies.

> Example: I bring the greatest value when I ensure my teams have access to

information and the autonomy to make decisions and experiment.

1) I bring the greatest value when I ...

2) I bring the greatest value when I ...

3) I bring the greatest value when I ...

Complete the sentences below: "You don't get the greatest value from me when ..."

> Example: You don't get the greatest value from me when my responsibilities include low-level operational functions like managing vendors.

1) You don't get the greatest value from me when ...

2) You don't get the greatest value from me when ...

3) You don't get the greatest value from me when ...

Complete the sentences below: "I lead with [x], so [y]."

> Example: I lead with empathy, so I am choosing to grant Howard three weeks

of extra paid bereavement leave.

1) I lead with [x], so [y] ...

2) I lead with [x], so [y] ...

3) I lead with [x], so [y] ...

Practice expressing your leadership like this. Get comfortable remembering your value and expressing it factually and calmly.

## Challenge 13: A Convenient Daily Reminder

Remember how Beth aced a high-stakes board interview she was nervous about when she printed out her catalyst statement and placed it in a visible spot to help remind herself of the unique value she brings? Take the time to collect the amazing work you've done thus far in this book so you can have a handy daily reminder of your value too.

Put it where you can see it regularly and use it as a touchstone to remind yourself of your F.A.R.E.™ leadership.

Here's an example:

**Tissa's Catalyst Statement**

I help leaders develop an unshakable sense of self so they can perform at their peak and lead values-based, high-performing teams.

**Tissa's Leadership Style**

I lead with empathy, curiosity, and transparency.

### Tissa's Leadership Values

I lead that way because I value respect, honesty, and ethics.

Now let's bring yours together.

My Catalyst Statement: *I bring the following value*

My Leadership Style: *I lead the following way*

My Leadership Values: *I lead that way because*

## Challenge 14: Go Live with Your F.A.R.E.™ Leadership

You've completed all the challenges in this book. The ones that await you now will be live challenges. Be the F.A.R.E.™ leader you've become. Activate your leadership, practice it daily, and always do the right thing. Have your values close at hand and top of mind so you can act quickly and confidently in every situation.

Don't be afraid to walk away or take an option off the table. Nothing is fatal or a failure. If you're making a decision based on your leadership values, you are making the right decision.

Use the space below whenever you need to work out a challenge. It will help you examine the situation with clarity so you can successfully live your leadership values. It will always be here for you as a guide. Return to it as often as you need to.

Describe a situation you are dealing with right now that impacts you or your team.

What are the stakes?

Which of your values is this situation challenging?

What scares you about speaking up? What do you think is at risk?

What is at risk if you DON'T do the right thing and lead with your values?

Write down your values talking points. How can you speak up in the situation and present your values as non-negotiable facts that don't need to be defended?

How did it feel to speak up and do the right thing? What was the result?

CPSIA information can be obtained
at www.ICGtesting.com
Printed in the USA
BVHW050402290323
661291BV00009B/538